Living Fre

Mark Emery

Mark Emery

Copyright © 2018 PCF World Mission LLC

All rights reserved.

ISBN-13: 978-0-578-41386-0

This book is a labor of love done for the hundreds of millions around the world who feel trapped, subdued and subjugated by a system which seems determined to suck any opportunity right out of life as soon as it appears. This work is a testimony to the blessings I've received and above all is dedicated to the power, glory and mercy of our lord Jesus the Christ who has similar and better blessings for all those who seek HIM.

Mark Emery

CONTENTS

	Introduction	i
1	What it's all about	1
2	The odyssey begins	13
3	How I became a 'Private Traveler'	42
4	How I became a 'Permanent Tourist'	51
5	How I became a 'Person of Talent'	58
6	How I became a 'Previous Taxpayer'	69
7	How I became 'Prepared Thoroughly'	75
8	Business & Banking for 'Proper Trade'	79
9	The Mystical Magical Suit - 'Preferably Teflon'	100
10	Freedom Begins with a 'Private Trust'	106
11	The Alt-Bank Solution for 'Preeminent Transactions'	114
12	Living without credit requires being 'Properly Trained'	128
13	Harmonizing law with 'Perfect Transcendence'	134
14	Living in 'Peaceful Tranquility'	159
15	Conclusion: This book is 'Prematurely Terminated'	162
16	Appendix	166

FORWARD

"Harriet Tubman once claimed that she freed a thousand slaves and could have saved a thousand more if only they knew they were slaves. That quote is even more relevant today than it was in the 1800s as nearly everyone on Earth today is now a slave... and most don't even know it. In this great book by Mark Emery he'll open to your eyes to your own slavery and hand you the key to unlock the prison all in one fell swoop."

- Jeff Berwick
  The Dollar Vigilante
  dollarvigilante.com

INTRODUCTION

As our Big Brother government (pick one) and its faceless, global, borderless, mega corporations combine to herd the people of the world into a digital web of surveillance, control and subjection, the flames of liberty and personal independence are being fanned like never before. In an age in which the concept of privacy is fast becoming little more than a quaint memory from our historical past, it is clear that the 'war is on' to dominate and control the people of the world. If we, as a free thinking independent populace intend to survive this war, we need to sharpen our acumen and skills in protecting and preserving our personal privacy and freedom.

Contrary to the global trends, strategies do still exist to achieve a level of personal freedom and privacy. Escaping the Matrix IS possible but it's not nearly as simple or easy as it once was just a few short years ago.

This book will prove it and give you some insights you just don't see anywhere. You'll explore some of those strategies and concepts in depth. As you read this book, you'll be riding shotgun as the author takes you with him around the world to experience the fun, the excitement and the success involved in being a 'free thinker' who had no desire in fitting into 'the mold'.

You'll also share some of the disappointments and failures which are ultimately necessary to forge us into the unbendable steel that we must become as we go into the world shining a light on the path to freedom and personal independence.

Much more than simply an academic study or a theoretical discussion, you'll read about the real life experiences of the author who is a 40 year practicing PT. He has been living what most would consider a 'dream life' having achieved his own freedom on many levels. But this only comes after paying a significant price with regular challenges and obstacles which he had to overcome with unshakable self determination, faith and bold action.

What you'll be reading about here is how he has done that often in ways that many could not imagine even possible let alone do-able. You'll gain some insights, tips and strategies which you've never heard of before nor will you find them being discussed anywhere else for a variety of reasons.

Successful people will attest to the fact bold action, intuitive instincts and intelligence acquired from personal experience provide the fuel for making quick, correct and important decisions 'on the fly' with bold confidence. You'll see examples of that in these chapters.

It is the hope and intention of the author that the result for you will be that you would gain renewed inspiration, hope and drive to get back on track to achieving your fullest God given potential with fewer if any restraints holding you down as they do now in our 'status quo' world.

Read….

Enjoy…

Follow the Path!

THE SECRET TO HAPPINESS IS FREEDOM... AND THE SECRET TO FREEDOM IS COURAGE.

- THUCYDIDES

1
WHAT IT'S ALL ABOUT

Who is really free?

Let's start with a very important question and the answer is not as simple as you may think. A reader of mine from the USA asked me once, "Why did you leave the states to live in Latin America?" I replied, 'Because I want to live free." He was taken aback by the immediate and simple reply and didn't quite know how to respond to that. Eventually he asked, "Well aren't we free in America?" With a question like that, I didn't even know where to begin or even 'if' I should begin. It would probably prove pointless.

However, for the benefit of all who are new to this concept and could use a little help, let's discuss this for just a minute and not a second more. Let me illustrate the situation with a little story.

So the slave master tells his slaves: "I'm going to pay you $100 a month if you work hard, don't get uppity and live a clean life and do as I say." You can't get married unless I say so. You can't leave the plantation unless I say so. You can't do anything else, unless I say so and I won't say so unless you give $1 to the family fund..

So the first month passes and it's time to pay his slaves. He gives each one $60. They look at each other confused. One gets up the nerve to ask, "But massa, you said you'd pay us $100. This is only $60." Master says, I DID pay you $100, *but had to deduct $40 to pay for your security around this place. I had to pay for your doctors visits. I know you didn't see the doctor but I have to pay him anyway just so he's ready for you when you need him. I need to pay for keeping the roads and machinery up around here so you can work and have a job and all kinds of other stuff!"*

So, pressed into financial hardship the slaves had to get creative and they did a little moonlighting at night to earn something extra. They'd get paid for the moonlighting job and they put it in a jar which they hid in their cabins on the plantation. One day the Master's foreman was inspecting the grounds and he found the jar. He informed the Master who decided to keep it.

The slaves found out and asked, "But Massa, we worked for that money. That's ours!" The Master came back, "everything on this plantation is mine and since you didn't report it to me or get my permission to do extra work, I'm keeping it. You should know better."

Now, without elaborating further, please tell me how you and your relationship to your boss and government and their collection agencies are any different than what these slaves are dealing with? Is there one iota of difference? Sadly no. Do you still feel free?

You don't own your home or your land. You only have 'Real Estate' which by definition is the 'conditional' right to use it. You do not have ownership. If you really owned it, why would you be paying annual 'rent' to the plantation owner to stay there? Stop paying 'rent' (real estate taxes) and see what happens. Your 'Massa' kicks you off of his land and takes it back. Is that 'ownership'? Where is your title to 'Land'? You don't have it.

You don't own your car. You only have a 'certificate of title' which is proof of private 'title insurance'. This is not ownership. If you really own your car, how can the plantation owner force you to pay to use your own car and then take it away from you if you violate too many of his rules? Simple. You paid for it, but it's not yours.

And get this. You don't even own your children. If you did, how could Child Protective Services just show up at your door and take your kids on a whim, without cause whenever they like? It happens every day and it's as dark and evil as it can be.

If you're lucky enough to be permitted to keep your children, your little girls and boys surely will not be allowed to set up a lemonade stand in the front yard without paying the Master $45 for a commercial vendors license! And if they did, they'd surely need to report earnings and pay the Master his 'fair share' of the earnings. Lemonade stands across the country are being shut down to squelch any spirit of entrepreneurialism our youngsters might have at an early age.

Do these examples seem extremely ridiculous to you? Well on one hand it is extremely ridiculous that people don't understand how the world works around them. But these are the cold hard facts and you'll learn more as we go along so have some patience and open your mind.

So no, you are not free. But the good news is that no slave works harder than the one who *'thinks'* he's working freely for himself and doesn't have a clue that he's a slave! So at least you might be able to enjoy the illusion of freedom, well, that is until you finish reading this book!

What Its means to be a PT

Do you want your Big Brother government to dominate and control every aspect of your life, your career, your finances and your property? PTs don't. They want to live an unfettered life of freedom and abundance to live on their terms, without any interference to fulfill their God given destiny.

The acronym 'PT' means different things to different people. It could represent: 'Private Traveller'. One who travels by right and not by license. It could mean 'Permanent Tourist' or 'Parked Temporarily', one who always appears to be from somewhere else wherever he is and has a corresponding level of immunity from local 'revenue enhancement' laws. A 'Person of Talent' is one who is always learning, advancing, developing and re-inventing himself and his business and investment portfolio, Someone who is 'Prepared Thoroughly' has an answer to most any situation which comes up. And the famous 'Previous Taxpayer' needs no explanation.

Whatever label you affix to it, it represents one thing alone in every case.... Mans desire to live FREE! It is in our inborn spirit which tells us to avoid those groups, institutions and systems which seek to control our every move and instead we should live free to be true to our own self to live and to seek our own God given destiny without hindrance.

Each one of those descriptive terms represents someone who wants to, or is, living free from the interference of third party interlopers in his life. Now at first glance, if you're not already familiar with the concept and all this is new to you, you surely have some pre-conceived notions by the mere mention of some of these terms. I urge you to put those notions aside for now and gain a better understanding of the depth and true meaning (not superficial) which is the purpose of writing this book for you.

Throughout history vast swaths of populations around the globe have been conned by leaders to give their undying allegiance, their money, their lives, their property and even their children to be sacrificed for the causes of those leaders and the purported higher values they espouse.

We can look at the same pattern appearing throughout the historical timeline as it relates to religious groups, political or national groups, fraternal groups, tribal or ethnic groups and the list goes on. And in each and every case, the 'subject volunteer' makes great personal sacrifice to advance 'the group'. What is the end result? 9 times out of 10 it ends in war, death and/or desolation. The 1 time out of 10 which is the 'aberration', the 'subject volunteer' is lucky to only suffer complete subjugation (lighter but effective forms of modern slavery) to the will of the group or the leader(s). Anyone who expresses any form of independent or critical thinking which doesn't conform to the 'group think' doctrine is punished severely or at best, vilified and outcast.

Let me prove this to you right now.

We all know that everyone must pay their (income) taxes, right? Everyone must pay their fair share! 'It's the law'!, they cry. It's common knowledge, right? Anyone who doesn't is scoffed at and ridiculed. Am I right? Then, as the story goes, they end up being punished severely with financial penalties, social exile, possible criminal charges and even jail time because everyone sitting in the jury box (not 'peers' by any stretch of the imagination) all pay their "fair share" of taxes and Lord knows, 'that's just the way it is'. (note: a jury of slaves will never let a free man go!)

Now, having established the common 'Group Think Syndrome' everything I mentioned above which most people 'believe' ...is a complete 'Con Job'. It's a confidence game which is perpetuated by the money powers to prop up their fraudulent system of domination and control (see my other books) . Through the propaganda of their institutions, controlled media and the collusion by the strongmen in the corrupt courts (collection agencies), they've perpetuated the con, enforced it and to this day people still overwhelmingly either believe it or at least conform due to 'fear'.

I've proven that it's a con. I'm living the alternative reality (in truth and law). I'll tell you more about the details later. Thankfully, many people are waking up to the fact that nearly everything we've been taught growing up is a lie. You'll understand better as we continue. Read on.

Individuality

In these days of public education, media manipulation of the truth and the resulting social pressure, finding people with the capacity for independent critical thinking is sadly becoming extremely rare. The social engineers have done a masterful job in turning the masses into lobotomized zombies. And on that subject, have you noticed in recent years the fascination with Zombie movies, video games, toys and other ways the 'Zombie' culture has been promoted, glorified and inserted into our society? They'd have you believe that being a Zombie is 'Cool'! And it's clear to see how that is happening. The social engineering is working.

After living abroad for some time, I returned to the states for a family visit. In my room I turned on the TV. I was absolutely stunned to see that every third ad on TV was for Big Pharma. In a 60 second ad they'd show an older couple frolicking with the family living the good life because they were on the designer drug of choice. This was the first 20 seconds. Then the remaining 40 seconds of the ad was a litany of side effects you should be wary of just in case you don't end up living the life of bliss this couple in the ad was living! "Some people have experienced chemical lobotomy, heart attack, stroke, bleeding from the eyes, nose and all orifices and/or have experienced extreme and prolonged diarrhea with uncontrollable bowels. But never mind that,

"Ask your doctor if this might be for you!"

Add to that the fluoridation of the water, the chemical and GMO poisoning of our food, chem-trails, public education and the leftist takeover (communist Chinese groups) of the university system which is indoctrinating helpless students on the wonders of 'socialism' and who are taught to look up to their teachers and not question 'the narrative' from a young age. Is it any wonder that we are surrounded by zombies!?

A wise individual will always look with skepticism and critical analysis upon any request for his time, money, devotion or allegiance and support to any cause, country, emperor, ruler, guru, nation, society or religion. I'm not saying we shouldn't give of ourselves. We should! Jesus is our example. But we should give to each other personally and when some group comes along waving a banner, we need to look very closely with a critical eye rather than just following blindly.

Here's a good example. People give blindly to the Red Cross and have for years. We see horrific images of suffering on TV of the latest hurricane victims and we send money to help. Little do you know that your donation is likely to be used for the reserve blanket supply in Hawaii and will never reach the Caribbean hurricane victims you intended to help. Do some research on the Red Cross scam. Take a look at the salaries of the executives and ask yourself if there's any better scam in existence? It'll be an eye opener. I don't give to Red Cross anymore.

But the point is, the astute individual who can think for himself and doesn't just fall in line with the fashionable 'group think syndrome' or propaganda of the moment will likely be looked at as a 'threat' to the power structure or the 'narrative' of the leaders or whatever group, and be vilified or cast out.

This is how our world works and is why 'Critical Thinkers' are so rare. 'Conformity' is now the highest form of morality. Individuality and the rejection of 'group values' are a toxic poison to the social engineers and are the cause of some of the most severe punishments. I'm personally fascinated by the history of the 'Cathars'. You've likely never heard of them. Look it up for a fascinating history lesson. Hint: How did the 'Inquisition' come about?

So, for the PT, he has rejected society's mold which is: get a degree, get a job, get a family with responsibility to tie you down, go into debt, file your taxes, pay your fees and fines, get permission to get married, get permission to travel to work, get permission to fix your gutters, pay for those permissions and pay more if you don't! Then pay for a car but never own it, pay three times the price of your house, but never own it, Be a debt slave the rest of your life and come into the corral like everyone else where you will likely die close to destitute so your progeny will have no inheritance and thus have no choice other than to follow in your footsteps into dependence and servitude.

A critically thinking 'PT' with a life of freedom, abundance and self preservation on his mind says 'Uh-Uh'. The crowd is going this way? I'm going 'that-a- way'. See ya!

But of course, people who think like that are a miniscule fraction of society. The vast majority are followers. They need someone to tell them what to do as in; a boss, a religious leader, a doctor, a teacher, a social media guru, a 'life coach', a therapist…. Anybody! Please! Just don't force me make my own decisions and be accountable or responsible!

If that's you, then this book is not for you unless perhaps you're doing research for a university paper on: DERELICTS

AND DELINQUENTS AND HOW THEY MUST BE PURGED FROM OUR ONE WORLD SOCIETY! Then I might be the perfect example for you to learn about. But aside from that, this book won't help you at all.

The Five Flag Strategy

Did you ever notice that visitors always get the red carpet treatment? When you visit someone's home they invite you in, offer something to drink, have a comfortable seat and you are always well attended for whatever you need. It's true isn't it?

The same is true when you travel. You arrive in another country. They welcome their visitors, give them assistance and are typically very friendly and willing to help in any way they can. Of course! You're likely a tourist or business visitor who is helping to support their economy. You have money to spend! What better reason to treat you with kid gloves?

In Panama they have 'Tourist Police'. No they're not there to bust your head open and haul you to court to get money out of you (like they are in one country I know of). They exist for one purpose only… to make the visiting tourists' stay as safe, secure and comfortable as possible. They are there to help you.

I could go on with the examples but you get the point.

Visitors from afar are welcomed with the red carpet, friendly smiles and any assistance or comfort they might need! So why wouldn't you want to get this kind of treatment all the time wherever you go wherever you are, even if you never go anywhere and stay right at home?

This is a no brainer right? A successful PT gets this treatment at home or wherever he might travel to. This, in addition to long term security are the primary objectives of the Five Flag Strategy.

What is the Five Flag Strategy?

1. You plant flag #1 in the country of your citizenship. This is represented by your passport.

2. You plant flag #2 in another country where you get a legal residence.

3. You plant flag #3 in another country where your business is domiciled (legally registered).

4. You plant flag #4 where you do your banking which is apart from all the others, and

5. You plant flag #5 in your playground where you like to spend most of your time and you have no ties whatsoever .

So here is what it looks like;

You carry an American/U.K./Australian or any other passport and show that for ID whenever you're out of the country. This works well because these countries are highly respected abroad (or in the case of the US, 'feared') and when officials see that, they generally don't want to mess with you and create an international incident. When you are in other countries, you are clearly a tourist when you show your passport.

You get a 'residence' with supporting ID in the country where flag #2 is planted. This will get you a government issued ID card and drivers license which can be very handy when you're in your home country or anywhere else dealing with roadside police stops or facing other types of liabilities which only apply to local residents. I'll expand on this later.

In your country of legal residence abroad, you show your passport when needed. You're a tourist. When you're at home you show your foreign resident card and drivers license. Again, you're a tourist no matter where you are.

The legal formation of the company you do business in, is in a third country. Why? You never want to do business in the country where you live or have your passport. Any issues or problems will haunt you and make your life potentially miserable if not outright dangerous. You will rarely go here, but when you do, you obviously appear as a 'tourist'.

The bank account for your company is in the fourth jurisdiction. Again, if your business ever gets attacked legally (and you don't have to do anything wrong for this to happen), they can't touch your bank account. Most banking is done via internet these days, unless it's some serious business so you'll rarely go here but when you do, you're a tourist!

You plant your fifth flag in the country where you like to spend most of your time. This is your playground. When you are here, all of your ties are elsewhere and you are clearly a 'tourist'.

End result: No matter where you are you appear to be a 'visitor', or foreigner. Remember that 'red carpet treatment' we talked about? You're covered.

At first blush this may appear to be quite expensive to set up. It's not really. Yes, you do need to travel a bit and spend some time, but hopefully you're doing that already anyway. If not, this gives you the perfect excuse to start taking some nice vacations! This is typically not something that is set up overnight. It's a strategy which is developed over time. Much like building a medieval fortress built to resist sieges...one brick at a time.

And you don't have to be planning to be a long term international traveller either. You can set yourself up once and be done with it and plan to sit tight and spend the rest of your years right at the old homestead.

Why would you do this? Why of course for a much higher level of privacy, protection and a certain level of immunity from the local 'revenooers'

What better situation could you ask for? You leave home to go on a few fun and interesting vacations and you come back a 'foreigner' in a teflon suit! Neat!

> *"EVERY HUMAN HAS FOUR ENDOWMENTS - SELF AWARENESS, CONSCIENCE, INDEPENDENT WILL AND CREATIVE IMAGINATION. THESE GIVE US THE ULTIMATE HUMAN FREEDOM... THE POWER TO CHOOSE, TO RESPOND, TO CHANGE."*
>
> *- STEPHEN COVEY*

2

THE ODYSSEY BEGINS

My love affair with foreign countries and cultures began in the fourth grade with my first French language class at St. Dominick's grade school in Northfield, Minnesota. Northfield is famous for its annual festival, the "Jesse James Days" where they re-enact a successful bank robbery pulled off by ol' Jesse and the James gang. You can still see some of the bullet holes in the bricks on the side of the old bank.

At this time in history The Monkees were all the rage and I was a huge fan! This was also the spark which got me going on playing guitar in rock-n-roll bands which I did for years, but that's off-point.

I was fascinated with how other cultures, in this case the French, could speak so differently, eat so differently and well, it seemed as though they lived in a different world. In those days they did! Those were the days before globalization took over and made retail, restaurants and hotels all basically the same product from one country to the next. In those days the local culture and tradition were distinct and predominant which, in fact, did make it a 'different world'.

I didn't have another chance to continue my French after 4th grade until I got into Junior High. I continued there from 7th grade all the way through senior year and then continued through several years of college with formal classes.

As a junior in High School my teacher Miss Papic got a burr under her saddle and decided we should all (the class) go to France! Heck, why not? Field trip! It took a little cajoling to get my parents to cough up the money to go, but they did and we all recognized it as a great opportunity and before long I was on my way to a 'foreign country'! Wow!

Remember, this was 1975 when the only means of communication back home or anywhere else was either by postcard or transatlantic telephone cable. So when you travelled abroad, you were really 'far away' and pretty much on your own. This was much unlike today when you can do selfies and send messages on WhatsApp anywhere in the world just like you do at home. It was a different time and I cherish having experienced that at that time.

It seemed like a long trip from Minneapolis to New York's JFK and then with a stopover in Iceland. We arrived in Paris tired and hungry. After checking in to the hotel a few of us decided to go out wandering the neighborhood to find something to eat. The hotel was in the neighborhood of the Notre Dame cathedral on Ile de La Cité. We stopped in a local pizza place which looked friendly enough and the food seemed 'safe' enough. I mean, how can you go wrong with a pizza? The menu was filled with words I didn't understand so I took a stab at it. "Je voudrais un pizza avec anchois" not having any idea what 'anchois' were. This was part of the adventure, right? I asked the waitress who tried to explain but it didn't help and I still didn't have a clue. It was my first meal in France and 7 years of French classes just went right out the window! But how can you go wrong with pizza, right? I went ahead with the order anyway.

So she finally arrived with the orders and she placed my 'pizza anchois' in front of me. To my absolute horror, I learned on the spot that 'anchois' is 'anchovies'! I was crestfallen. I was anticipating a wonderful pizza to satisfy my hunger after a long trip but NOT this! I can eat just about anything, but anchovies are definitely not on the list. I picked them off the pizza and suffered through the rest of the meal with the residual tainted flavor they left behind despite the fact that they were removed. It was a very anti-climatic start to my first French experience.

The French eat all kinds of very weird things including some very strange sea creatures. I was invited to a family Christmas celebration some time later, and the primary festive family dish was brought out on a large platter. It was clear that the entire gathering was eagerly anticipating this rare delicacy which they were about to enjoy. The cook came out with a large platter. On It was some kind of white meat all coiled up serpentine like and I was truly scratching my head thinking, 'what on God's green earth could this possibly be?'

They passed the platter around and everyone eagerly took their portion. It came to me and it was still a complete mystery what it was. I'm thinking, 'When in Rome do as the Romans', right? So I took my portion and found the courage to ask "what is this?". It was 'eel'. OohhKayyy then....

Honestly, I had some very serious reservations but I succumbed to the cultural pressure and got past the mental block to try it. Honestly, once I tasted it, It was just like white fish and quite good really. I replaced the mental image with a Sea Bass, and everything was fine from that point on.

But you commonly find restaurant menus offering organ meats like kidney and liver even headcheese or worse. I quickly learned to develop my personal preferred menu choices and until I had the French menu mastered, it was always an easy order of 'Steak frites, bien cuit' every time. Steak and fries well done was the old standby for many a meal. When in doubt, it's 'Steak frites, bien cuit!'

Another similar event occurred as I recall going out with a group of friends for lunch when I was living in Aix-en-Provence in my college days. In France, lunch is not 'lunch' as we know it. It's a grand affair which you should schedule about 2 hours to partake in and at least 2 hours after to recover from. The good restaurants have a 'prix fixe' or fixed price menu and the chef prepares one menu for everyone and you get what he has prepared for the day.

First comes the bread and wine with a dish of balsamic vinegar and olive oil for the bread. Then maybe a little assortment of prosciutto or cold meats to snack on with canapes. Then comes a fantastic salad. After that comes a Vichyssoise cold leek soup followed by a hot salmon soufflé. I know you're thinking, 'Wow what a great meal!'. I said that once after about three courses and said, "That was great! I'm full!" People looked at me from under furrowed brows like I just arrived from another planet. "No. We're not done yet!"

Then comes a little ball of 'sorbet' to cleanse the pallet before the main course which could be Boeuf Bourguignon or Duck a l'Orange, or Coq-au-vin or a Seafood Paella, you get the idea.

So after this fine culinary and cultural event (déjeuner) for us green eared kids, the waitress asks if we'd like anything else. I said 'Mais oui'. I was thinking of an after dinner liqueur like a Courvoisier brandy or a Grand Marnier or Cointreau. I was going to be suave and debonair in front of all my friends. I had heard of (what I thought was) a Liqeuer which I had never tried before. So, feeling curious and bold, I ordered 'Chantilly'. The waitress looked puzzled and asked, "Really? That's all? Would you like it with anything else or just by itself?" And she was still looking very puzzled. I confidently replied without hesitation, 'No. Just by itself of course!', thinking to myself that aficionados with sensitive palates like myself only enjoy the finer things in their purest form! Naturally, you don't want to pollute your senses when enjoying the unique and pristine, multi-sensual experience you get from a delicacy or any flavor by mixing it with any other substances. That's sacrilege in France! You just don't do that. To fully enjoy any cuisine, for example, you cannot mix the food. To do so is a huge insult to the chef. It shows that you are not taking the proper care to fully envelope your senses with the experience that the chef has meticulously prepared. Thus each plate is served separately and you cleanse the palate with sorbet before enjoying the final crowning main course achievement of the chef.

So, moments later the waitress brought out my very special Chantilly. Strangely enough, it was not quite what I expected. What she brought out was a HUGE mixing bowl from the kitchen full of whipped cream all fluffy and fresh and she put it down on the table in front of me. The entire table just erupted in ferocious laughter that didn't stop for 10 minutes I swear! We were in tears. So much for being 'suave and debonair'!

So the point is that you don't have that kind of fun and adventure eating 'lunch' at the Olive Garden or Burger King!

Exploring new cultures can be a bit intimidating especially if you don't speak the language well. But it can give you memorable experiences you'd never get anywhere else.

French Police: My First Win as a 'PT'!

I'm still on my first high school trip to France staying with a French family and I'm with Pierre, the son of the family who took me in for a few days and served me the eel for Christmas. Pierre is my age. They live just down the road from the Palace of Versailles. Versailles is a suburb of Paris. It was a dark, cold day of drizzle which is typical in the French winter.

Pierre and I were getting cabin fever and so we each went out to grab a Mobylette (Moped scooter) from the garage and he's taking me out on an adventure despite the weather.

We head down a busy main street in Versailles to the gardens of the Palace of Versailles which are immense and almost endless. Mobylettes are prohibited from entering the gardens precisely to prevent the likes of us from entering and doing exactly what we were about to do, race around mindlessly tearing up the gardens. Neither the prohibition nor the signs slowed us down a bit. Pierre knew just where to get in unnoticed.

The wet weather made it a perfect day to be spinning donuts and the dark drizzly day gave us perfect cover with limited visibility. Plus, the weather kept most tourists away on this day so we had the vast manicured gardens to ourselves.

Pierre would take off and I'd do my best to catch him weaving in and out of terraced gardens, fountains and across manicured lawns. When I did catch up with him, he'd spin around and take off in another direction and the chase was on again. My dogs do this when they play with each other. It's pretty much the same thing.

After a couple of hours of Mobylette mayhem we were low on gas and up to our ears in mud and thought it best to get out while the 'gettin'' was still good.

So we exited the Palace gardens and headed back out on the streets for home. Pierre was ahead of me as I followed so he didn't notice when I was pulled over by the French police for not having a light on such a dark and rainy day. The light didn't work anyway we both found out, so that was a moot point which made it a perfect scenario for the police to get some quota points and issue me a ticket.

He was adamant that he was not going to let me go until he got my ID to give me a ticket.

Pierre finally turned around and saw what was going on and circled back. After he and I both made it abundantly clear to the policeman that I was not French, but a foreigner, he finally relented and let me off with a warning and away I went.

This was my first victory over officialdom as a teenage, renegade 'PT' and at that time I had no clue as to what a 'PT' even was! It was accidental and not intentional (as later encounters would be) but it was real. I just had the experience and it left its mark.

IBLAS & Aix-en-Provence

So my high school trip to France opened my eyes to the big world of international language, culture and lifestyle opportunity. This experience pointed me in the direction of seeking a Bachelors degree in International Business and Language Area Studies (IBLAS) at St. Norbert College in DePere, Wisconsin (Green Bay area) which was one of only 2 or 3 such specialized International business degrees or curriculums available in the country at the time (1976). Today they are much more plentiful.

During my four years in the program I continued my study of the French language and ended up spending six months living in France as I attended the Institute for American Universities (I.A.U.) there in Aix-en-Provence as a part of the program.

Aside from being just an overall enchanting life experience living in the 'city of fountains' in southern France, one of the more notable experiences revolved around my involvement with the Le Baron family. Monsieur Francois Le Baron and his wife came to my university one day looking for someone to come out to his place on weekends to teach his young son English. It would be a cultural experience for the volunteer and a great learning opportunity for his son. Somehow, I happened to walk by the administrators office at just the right time and ended up as the volunteer.

Monsieur Le Baron (Francois) had a cheese truck (how fortunate for me being a Green Bay Packer fan otherwise known as 'Cheeseheads' - Wisconsin is known as America's Dairyland in case you didn't know) . He would travel a set circuit every week and take his cheese truck to quaint farmers markets in ancient medieval villages throughout the countryside of southern France. I travelled with him a couple of times and loved it. I couldn't count the variety of cheeses he offered but I can say with absolute certainty that some of them sure didn't smell very good!

The French have always been completely infatuated with the old American western movies. You know, John Wayne, Clint Eastwood, Gunsmoke and the like. They have this image of all Americans as cowboys who drink whiskey and smoke Marlboro cigarettes. That's the typical iconic American stereotype for many French to this day.

So Monsieur Le Baron had this same image in his mind as it related to me. He taught me, or I could even say 'forced' me to start drinking whiskey so I could fit his stereotype. I was only 20 at the time and had not yet developed my palette for whisky and frankly couldn't stand the stuff. But since I was (in his mind) an American cowboy, he would frequently approach me asking if I wanted a whiskey. I would politely decline time after time and he didn't seem to get the idea I really didn't want it. Well, he stopped asking me and started just bringing it to me. His determination to give me a whiskey apparently was greater than my determination not to take it, and finally, to appease him, I started drinking it merely to be a gracious guest and not be rude. The first couple of drinks were absolutely horrible. But I soon learned the art of sipping and savoring the flavor and absorbing it in my olfactory receptors and thanks to this persistent, cowboy loving Frenchman, I'm now a fanatical whiskey lover! Although thankfully, I never caught on to smoking Marlboros or roping cattle!

These are the cultural dilemmas one encounters in the international life. Let's segway over to politics.

Rabble Rousing at the University

I was studying at the Institute for American Universities in 'Aix' at that time. I.A.U. was small and it catered to Americans as the name would indicate. There was also a very large public university in town where several thousand French students attended.

The two universities planned a cultural exchange between student groups and the French 'Aix' University students came over to see us at our place for the event.

We eventually ended up discussing politics and the differences between France and the USA. In those days French President Valery Giscard d'Estaing, a moderate conservative had recently given the reigns of the government over to Francois Mitterrand, an open and avowed socialist who was just coming into power as the new French President.

I made the comment to the group that "the French never like to admit it, but their government is clearly headed to socialism." The French group was aghast that I would make such a declaration. This was akin to insulting Edith Piaf, the historically famous French singer. Sacrebleu!

They fervently denied having any semblance to socialism and vehemently defended themselves as NOT being socialist. I needed only reply to them that; "Look at the facts... the government owns the main TV channels and broadcasting companies, the government owns the universities and subsidizes the students, the government owns Electricite´ de France (EDF) which owns the nuclear power industry in France and provides nearly all electricity. The government owns Aerospaciale a state-owned aerospace manufacturer that builds both civilian and military aircraft, rockets and satellites. The government owns the national railway company the SNCF and provides its citizens with government run health care and pension systems. Government is involved in nearly every aspect of life in France. How is that not Socialism?

I had to explain to them that François Mitterand himself was elected as a member of the *Parti Socialiste* when he won the Presidency of France in 1981 the Socialists had achieved domination of the politics of France at the time. The municipal elections of 1977 had given Socialists unprecedented local control of cities and the 1981 national elections, in addition to electing Mitterand, gave Socialists a majority in the National Assembly, the legislature of France.

I asked, how can you say that France is not heading in the socialist direction unless you say that they have already arrived? The room went silent. I had just cracked the popular myths that people were holding onto and forced them to take a red pill for a time. I've been at it ever since.

It was clear that the students whom I was talking to had no clue as to what was really going on or what reality was. They had apparently been brainwashed by their government controlled media way back then and were flabbergasted when someone like me came along, a foreigner not affected by the government media, and burst their bubble.

This is exactly what we see going on today all over the world including countries with a strong heritage in liberty and freedom such as Australia, Canada and the United States. The majority of people themselves refuse to see reality for what it is. And that reality is that they are currently living in various advanced forms of creeping socialism in their daily lives today and they don't even see it! They'll deny it to the end and ultimately be swallowed up in it if they're not already.

Amazing!

This experience with the French students taught me how people become willfully blind. When offered the plain truth they refuse it because it upsets their belief system and with that, their personal identity and world view.

If for this reason alone and no other, it validated my quest to separate myself from 'the crowd' and find my own way in this world so I could preserve my own critical thinking ability and in so doing, preserve my own chances for 'self preservation'. This attitude alone would save me many times over.

This confirms what my father told me on numerous occasions which was: "The masses are asses. Think for yourself!" Right on dad!

My question to myself, to you and others is simple: "How can one live a life built on lies and not want to know the truth?" Sadly most people do. Not me!

It was at this point that I achieved the 'PT' level of *'Proactive Thinker'!*

Back to 'The Real World'!

So back at St. Norbert College and the IBLAS program where I spent my last semester after returning from France, my class was importing handicrafts from Central America through a black market channel we had set up. We were selling the handicrafts to help fund campus charity projects.

Our import business was a project in the IBLAS program to learn the ins and outs of importing goods. St. Norbert being a Jesuit college (quasi Catholic) there were many priests on campus, they were in faculty, administration and involved in everything. We identified and contacted some priests who travelled to Central American missions and co-opted them to be used as mules to bring us back boxes of goods we could sell. This way we completely avoided much of the red tape (taxes) and bureaucracy on commercially imported goods.

So I have the friars at St. Norbert College to thank for giving me my first lesson in how to position yourself properly so that the taxes and regs don't always apply to you! What college have you ever heard of which would teach you that with actual hands on experience? I was impressed!

Recruited by the Pros

Well, despite my dreams to the contrary, my dedicated 10 year career in football had its moments but didn't end in any professional gridiron glory after playing intensely from little league through college.

But my professional career in business sure started with a bang! With my background and experience, I was shooting for a job in international business of course.

A long story short, I answered an ad I saw in the Chicago Tribune where I was living at the time and the ad was clear that this international company was seeking someone with a Masters degree in international business (which I didn't have). I only had a Bachelors degree. They also wanted 5 years corporate international experience minimum (which I didn't have). The job was 'Area Market Manager' to develop distribution for the company's consumer products in Europe and Africa.

This was the dream job that I figured would take me at least 5 to 10 years to work into starting as a fresh grad. I took a flyer on it, answered the ad and got invited for an interview.

As it turned out, after much deliberation and delay I got the job. I was ecstatic! The way I figured it, the company had set their sights high with the requirements they were seeking and like I said earlier, in those days degrees in international business were rare. To find an MBA in that niche with five years or more of overseas experience might have been a bit of a stretch or wishful thinking.

Here I came along, with excellent French language skills to get me through most of North Africa Arab nations and West African nations which were largely ex French and British colonies. Plus, I actually had experience living overseas and with those qualifications I likely surpassed other candidates who applied. Then, being a fresh grad they could get away with paying me much less than what they were advertising for and they got a lot more value!

So, the bottom line was that they found an excellent free agent with top skills and experience and they were able to stay well under the salary cap! It wasn't quite what I had envisioned as a kid playing football, but still, I was off to the pros in a different league!

Dumped in the Scrub Brush

I'll never forget taking my first trip to Africa on an 'Air Afrique' airlines which doesn't exist anymore. We were on final approach moments before touch down in Dakar, Senegal. It was my first stop on a direct flight from JFK in New York.
I was looking out the window and all I saw was sun

bleached dirt and scrub brush on the African plain. I remember it as plain as day, like it was yesterday. I was thinking to myself, "Geez Mark. Here you are in the bushland of Africa. What the hell have you done now?"

Prior to that, the first several months on the job were spent preparing for and planning the trip. I was translating the product catalog and brochures into French. I was researching the major importers and distributors in the key cities in Senegal, Liberia, Ivory Coast, Cameroon and Nigeria mostly. Nigeria was the main target as it was the most populous and richest country in West Africa being an oil producer and member of OPEC.

Then my boss Ali Khan, who was a serious but delightful Pakistani, basically said, OK Mark you're ready to travel. Here's your expense account, tickets etc. and don't come back until you sell something! And off I went ready for anything! And it was a good thing too as 'Anything' was quite likely to happen as I was about to find out.

The company I worked for was EKCO Housewares. You probably recognize the name and have some of their products in your home. People in social gatherings would often ask me what I did. My short reply was, "Oh, I sell pots and pans in Africa!'. And I swear the image people would have in their minds upon hearing that was to imagine me with a large sample case strapped to my back, scurrying from grass hut to grass hut trying to sell my wares on the Serengeti. Not quite.

A little closer to reality was that I would try to configure orders and sell the product by the container load. I'd deal with chain stores, grocery and department stores, importers and distributors some of whom had their home offices in London or Paris where I'd occasionally visit to meet the top brass to launch new product promotional campaigns or just try to schmooze them for a large order.

In order to secure payment in dollars when the country had its own national currency (like the Nigerian Naira) I'd have to arrange an irrevocable letter of credit from an international bank which was confirmed by a bank in the USA. This led me into some interesting meetings in banking and politics as the two are inextricably intertwined.

So getting the order was one thing. But it was only the first step. In the case of Nigeria and a couple others, then you'd have to apply for a permit from government to be allocated the US dollars to send from the country's foreign currency reserves in the central bank. There was 'no sale' until that happened.

Corruption in Nigeria

With all of the oil and investment money floating around Nigeria, corruption in politics had permeated everything. As in most places, getting elected to office was the equivalent of getting a license to steal. Add to that the historical tribal tensions which have always existed throughout history between the three main tribes there and which persist to this day and you have a formula for some real problems.

Nigerians still identify with their tribes. So much so, that each tribe has their own 'mark' to permanently identify its members. They scar their face with a specific pattern of stripes or marks which identified the tribe so it would be permanent and obvious to all which tribe one belonged to. There was no 'switching parties'!

So I was doing my thing on another trip to Adventureland. I had arranged a huge order which would make me a superstar with my EKCO team. In the hotel bar I had run into a wild eyed Irishman named Kelly who was a wheeling dealing Tasmanian devil and he fell in love with our broad lines of products. He came up with a plan to place orders for 40 container loads to be distributed throughout a network of clients he had. This was huge.

At the time, the central bank of Nigeria was located in the national telecommunications building which was a prominent and new high-rise office building. With the new orders all lined up I was preparing to head to the central bank with the Kelly that week to apply for the foreign currency exchange permits.

It just so happened to be election season in Nigeria at the time. Of course, during their tenure the politicians in office at the time were actively sending millions of dollars of ill gotten gains from corruption to their personal accounts in Switzerland which still had a modicum of privacy in those days. With the new regime soon to be coming into office after elections, they had to cover their tracks (sound familiar?). So what was the best way to do this? Of course! Burn the entire national bank building down. What else?

National telecommunications were down. Banking was down. The country came to a halt. But for the corrupt politicians, at least their money was safe in Switzerland!

In writing this, I did a couple searches real quick on the topic and damn, if they hadn't done it again just as recently in May of 2018 ! Hey, It must work!

Don't we see the Democrats in the USA doing the same thing today in 2018-2019 using 'Bleach Bit' and hammers to hard drives? They're burning the country and its institutions down figuratively without any concern for the collateral damage they create just to save their asses from the Trump truth tribunals. It's the same playbook. I never thought I'd see people in my home country stooping to the level of the tribal animals as I saw in Nigeria, but here we are.

Scotch & a Wild Irishman - Stimulates Creative Thinking

This order I was working on was too important to just 'let go' due to circumstances. I needed to solve this problem. So I got back with Kelly the wild Irishman to do some brainstorming. It took a couple bottles of good Scotch over a few nights to fuel the creative think tank but it did the job and after some serious configurations and some good laughs, the result was in.

We arrived at a solution using countertrade. Countertrade is the international exchange of goods rather than cash. This would be tricky though because I knew EKCO had no interest in being terribly creative. Cash was the only solution for us to ship product.

So here's how the deal went down.

The Nigerian importers (our customers) would arrange to sell goods they had access to, to a German client Kelly had. The amount of the sale of goods would equate roughly to the amount of goods to be shipped from EKCO in Chicago to Nigeria. This took some time to configure. We'd have to sell the idea to qualified players. Not an easy task.

Through nothing short of a miracle, we found the players and they were game. A letter of credit in favor of EKCO would be lodged by the German importer whereby before having funds released to EKCO, the Nigerian client's shipment would have to arrive in Germany in acceptable condition, and then EKCO would receive the bank advice whereupon EKCO would ship it's goods to Nigeria knowing that all the preconditions have been met and the money for payment was sitting in the German bank awaiting delivery.

Upon receipt of the EKCO shipment in Nigeria, the German bank would be notified and then release funds to EKCO. So instead of the German buyer paying the Nigerian for his goods, he'd pay EKCO that amount and the Nigerian would receive payment for his shipment to Germany not in cash but in goods from EKCO which he could then sell for a nice profit.

Naturally, this is not something you do every day, but for an order of 40 container loads, it was worth the effort.

Bear this situation in mind if ever confronted with a cash shortage and you really want to sell something!

Somehow I can't help but think that my friend Francois LeBaron who introduced me to fine Scotch whiskey back in France had a hand in this! This was 'proof' that 'everything happens for a reason'.

Liberia Rolls Out the Red Carpet

The first business meetings I had in Africa were in Monrovia, Liberia. Monrovia is an interesting place. Named after the US President James Monroe in 1816, with the aim of establishing a self-sufficient colony for emancipated American slaves, something that had already been accomplished in Freetown, Sierra Leone, the first settlers arrived in Africa from the United States, under the auspices of the American Colonization Society. They landed at Sherbro Island in present-day Sierra Leone.

Naturally, American influence here is strong and the country of Liberia to this day functions on the US dollar as its currency. I loved this because no foreign currency permits were needed! Just make the order and set up the L/C with the bank.

Most of the more successful businessmen in Liberia were either from Lebanon or India. Lebanon at the time was still feeling the effects of a vicious civil war which turned it from a luxurious modern coastal paradise on the Mediterranean to a dangerous heap of rubble. Many of the merchants escaped to other places where they could do business in peace. Liberia was one of those places being a gateway to West Africa.

The Indians were very prevalent along with the Lebanese and both groups were most gracious hosts. I've had nothing but wonderful experiences with the great people from India and Lebanon, wherever I was in the world. They'd invite me in to their private quarters in the back room which were luxurious and quite unexpected from the dingy outward appearances of their place. I'd be seated on fine upholstered French colonial style furniture. The floor was covered with a work of art in the form of a Persian rug with exquisite tapestries on the wall. They'd offer me anything I'd like to drink and I usually settled for their famous Turkish coffee. We'd talk about the world, culture, global and local politics, the general business climate and more.

While drinking their strong Turkish coffee, not only did I learn to love it but I learned their custom of reading the dried coffee grounds to tell your future. Let me explain. When finished with the coffee, you turn the small porcelain cup over and let the coffee grounds which remained in the cup, slide down onto the plate. When they dried, it was the custom for certain soothsayers to be able to read the pattern left in your dried coffee to tell you things about yourself and your future, much like a palm reader. I love strong coffee and fell in love with this Turkish coffee, Lebanese style!

Beyond the in-suite hospitality, they'd offer me one of their cars and a personal driver during my stay so I wouldn't have to humble myself in the dirty taxis that ran through the city.

I felt like a king. All of this would occur before we'd even start to talk about business. By that time, we had developed such a friendship the business was almost an afterthought and pretty much automatic.

It was through experiences like this which taught me early on that being the 'visitor from afar' had some very distinct advantages. I could get used to this!

Pulling Rank in Morocco

I had planned a long trip for North Africa which started in Morocco then led to Algeria, Libya, Tunisia and finally Malta. I had a very detailed and complex itinerary meticulously laid out and prepared down to the last detail which took quite some time to arrange. Arranging all the flights, hotels and meetings took me several weeks to accomplish. This was going to be an important trip.

So my flight lands in Casablanca, my first stop. Before I even checked in to the hotel I learned that the muslim holiday of Ramadan was just beginning and the country literally shuts down during the day. How could this happen? How could I be in communication with so many people about the trip and nobody even mention this? My entire schedule was shot to hell. I had to start over but I was already in Casablanca. Now what?

Man! Where is that Scotch when you need it? The odds of finding Scotch whiskey in a muslim country during Ramadan are about the same as stumbling into a forest fire in the Arctic. It ain't gonna happen!

So what's the only thing to do when you can't do business for a few days? Have fun of course! I decided take advantage of the opportunity and go on a little tour of the country. I rented a car and made the drive of several hours from Casablanca on the highway down to see the historical and exotic Marrakech.

This was the very first time I had ever rented a car in a foreign country. Some of the road signs included some French which I could understand, but many of them were only in Arabic so my navigation relied largely on instinct and luck with the help of a roadmap I bought. It was a bit nerve-racking.

But the trip down to Marakech made me feel like I had gone through a time warp to travel several centuries back in time.

Out on the open road I had passed an old man with his camel pulling a bucket of water out of a well with the rope tied to the camel. This was in front of a small ancient village out in the middle of nowhere which was encircled by a mud packed wall. I didn't see an electric line anywhere.

There were various instances of camels roaming free on the barren countryside. I had spectacular views of the Atlas Mountains off in the distance.

Finally I arrived in Marrakech just outside the 'old city' which was walled in from ancient days. A young kid saw me get out of my car and instantly recognized me as a foreigner which was an opportunity for him. He convinced me to let him be my tour guide and it was a good decision. It was the best five bucks I've ever spent.

He took me into the back rooms, back streets and the belly of the ancient city and I saw it in a way that probably few ever have. We walked casually through a back private room where a group of old Moroccan men in their traditional Arab garb were sitting on the floor around a water pipe (Shisha/Houkah) and smoking whatever it was they were used to smoking. I got a whiff and had a pretty good idea.

I remember seeing an old man sitting, practically sleeping, on his burro which carried him and some packs one step at a time through a narrow passage way. I was looking over my shoulder expecting to see Humphrey Bogart. It was a scene from a time gone by, except it was today!

Then came the bazaar full of merchants selling their beautiful copper ware, rugs, tapestries, woodworks, and you name it. It was there and the products were beautiful.

In the common public square it was a free for all with a variety of sights, sounds and smells. I saw an old man sitting on a very small stool in a tattered suit. He looked to me like a drunk trying to recover from the night before. He had a blanket laid out with various instruments on it and a few bottles of colored liquid. I asked my guide, 'Who is this guy? What does he do?" He replied, 'Oh he's a dentist. He can fix your teeth!'. At that point in time I was eternally grateful that I didn't have a toothache.

Then there was a guy talking to a big crowd gathered around him. I asked about him. "Oh he's a story teller. He tells good stories and people give him tips.

And of course the story wouldn't be complete without the snake charmers. Yes, There was an actual snake charmer there with 2 cobras. He kept them under a lid and when I came up to them they'd lift the lid and handle the snakes. He let me take a picture but of course that cost me a small fee.

So, I head back to Casablanca and get caught up in traffic which was terrible as people seemed to be going in every which direction without any order. Another little surprise which snuck up on me was the fact that, if the signs being in Arabic weren't enough of a hardship, the city had just changed all the circulation patterns in the city streets so even the local people were disoriented and ended up going the wrong way when they went the way they were accustomed to going which wasn't correct anymore. It was a mess.

I was due to leave the next day and was happy about that even though I had the experience of a lifetime in Marrakech.

On my way to the airport I was going down a narrow one way street and noticed a police officer pulling several cars over to the side ahead of me. I tried to pass and he insisted I pull over as well.

We were all going down a one way street the wrong way. Just last week it was a two way street so even the local people were being caught off guard.

I finally realized that the cars he was pulling over ahead of me were being towed away and I started to panic. The police confirmed that I would have my turn with the tow truck as well. I was on my way to drop the rental car off and catch a flight. I had no time for this falderal.

I had to think fast and get out of this mess. I started trying to talk logic to him. Didn't work. He didn't care about logic. I pleaded with him to have mercy on a foreigner. Nope. He didn't care. He was making money for the city and would surely be applauded for his efforts. He wasn't budging.

Finally I started to raise my voice and get irate. I took my passport out and flashed it for him and I said, 'Do you know what this is? It's a US passport. I work for the U.S. Embassy as a special attaché'. I opened my passport book to flash my credentials (which was nothing) in front of him really fast as if to prove my status. He didn't challenge me on it. The bluff worked.

I started ranting and raving that he already had plenty of 'customers' but that he didn't want me because I had a high level meeting at the Moroccan presidential palace I was expected to attend and if he was responsible for detaining me any longer, he could be held responsible for an international incident. I went on along this theme and made it clear that he was clearly outranked in this situation and after I started asking for his information and ID he realized that the easiest thing to do would be to let me go rather than face the potential consequences I had built up in his mind. Key point: I did not willingly submit to his authority and I asserted my own by taking control of the situation.

I didn't wait for or ask for his approval. I made my point very clear in a strong and confident posture and affirmatively 'assumed the close' praying that my bluff would work. It did. I got in my car and he let me drive away. I got the car back to the agency and got to the airport on time.

This little escapade taught me a little bit about psychology and how by combining a little bit of dramatic theatrical flair along with my American passport, a little confident creativity could go a long way!

I felt totally in control of my own destiny and this victory put the icing on the cake for a wonderful adventure with fond memories of Morocco.

My foundational field training to be a 'PT' was well underway!

Finally! Homeless at Last!

My job with EKCO had run its course in Chicago and I ultimately decided that climbing the corporate ladder wasn't for me. I didn't like office politics and the required conformity to the corporate culture so I broke free and went out on my own as a business broker.

With my international background, the C.I.A. had found me and was actively recruiting me. Out of curiosity I played along with them until the last minute before I backed off the process. No way was I going to sacrifice my life working on government scale. More on that subject in my other book mentioned below.

I moved from Chicago to Denver where I started to learn first hand about tyranny and government abuse of power. I started studying the law intensely and developed myself into a professional troublemaker with my newly acquired knowledge of the law. I got my own radio show focusing on these subjects and caused enough heartache with the local crooks that I spent a year in prison as my reward. This was one of the best years of my life. You can read all about that in my other book:

ONE FREEMANS WAR
IN THE SECOND AMERICAN REVOLUTION.

Upon release from parole I moved to Oklahoma, just a block from the bomb site of the Federal Murah Building. I got married to an Oklahoma girl and she had a little 'Yorkie' Yorkshire terrier who was a real cutie.

My independence had allowed me to make more than I ever had previously as an employee and I was blessed to be able to buy a 37' Itasca motorhome with two slide out sections. It was beautiful. This was in 1998 and the ultimate objective here was in planning for the big Y2k meltdown scare everyone was talking about in those days. If you're too young to remember that, it was said that the computers were not properly programmed to roll over from dates in the 1900s to the 2000s and that nearly all computers could go haywire and possibly put us back into the dark ages.

I wanted to be mobile and thus bought the motorhome.

We maintained a small apartment in Oklahoma City (OKC) and when I pulled up to the apartment complex for the first time in that luxury land yacht, a feeling of excitement and pending adventure started welling up inside of me which I couldn't hold back. We got it provisioned and equipped and were ready to head out on the open road.

From OKC I first headed to Colorado for a family gathering in the mountains. The house where my family was staying was full and overflowing with family and kids. I was very happy to have brought 'my own place' with me and we even had room for a couple of kids from the overflow. It was so nice having a comfortable peaceful spot to get away from the crowd.

On the way back we found a spectacular campsite to park and spend the night, right on Grand Lake. The RV was parked in amongst the pines looking right out over the lake. It was heaven.

The following day I climbed Trail Ridge road and crossed the Continental Divide on the way to Estes Park. I remember taking in the spectacular views and thinking that this was just too beautiful to just drive through and pass by. So I found the perfect place to park the RV up on a perch on top of the world and we soaked in the incredible beauty while we had a relaxing lunch which we were in no hurry to finish. I was getting used to this mobile lifestyle believe it or not!

My wife had relatives she wanted to see in the Ozarks so we headed over to see them in Eureka Springs and stayed in a gorgeous spot in the hills there before heading over to Branson to see a couple shows, again staying amongst the pines in the fresh air of a national forest.

All the while, I was towing a beautiful white and gold Jeep Grand Cherokee behind the RV so we could get out and explore each local area or city we came upon with ease.

Next stop was Chicago to see my aunt and her family. She lived on the north shore so I found a beautiful spot in the

Illinois Beach State Park right on Lake Michigan to park 'the rig'. Aside from the curious skunk who wanted to share our space with us for a time, we had a great visit with Maren and her family before heading up to Door County, Wisconsin.

Along the way, as we approached Green Bay I stopped at my alma mater St. Norbert College and walked the grounds stirring up fond memories from the college days and seeing what was new after 20 years.

It was fall, and I had my sights set on getting to a Packer game even though I had no tickets. Lambeau Field was just a couple miles down the road from St. Norbert College.

But first we headed north to the peninsula and arrived in Door County. We encountered a spectacular display of nature, history and culture. The beautiful fall colors were setting in on the trees. We attended a famous Door County 'fish boil dinner' which was a dramatic cultural and culinary event. But the important event for me was the Sunday Packer game against the arch rival Vikings coming up in a couple days.

Sunday morning arrived and we headed to the stadium parking early in search of tickets. Ha! Tickets to the Viking game? Are you kidding? Dream on, right? I circled the stadium several times and found nothing!

I did find a scalper asking ridiculous amounts for his tickets and passed, holding that option as an absolute last resort. I'd wait until kickoff time if I had to, when the price comes crashing down. But in the meantime I kept searching.

I went to the 'Will Call' ticket window and they had nothing and the girl shot me down. I was just standing there off to the side pondering my next move when a guy came up to the window to get his tickets which were set aside for him to pick up. He asked the price and apparently was not

prepared to pay what they were asking for them and he walked away. I asked the clerk in the window, "Hey, are those tickets available?". She replied, 'Yes'. I was in!
Not only was I 'In' but these were Sky Box seats for only $103 each! I was like a dog rolling in clover! This was a miracle!

Living in luxury in the Sky Box with waiter service watching the game live and from all angles with replays on the TVs all around us in the midst of the energy from the crowd at Lambeau Field could only be matched by the finish to the game.

The Vikings just scored a critical touchdown late in the fourth quarter to take the lead in a tight, hard fought game. The Packers were now behind by 4 points and needed a touchdown with only a minute left on the clock when they got the ball back for a last ditch effort. It looked bleak for the Packers. It was the ultimate pressure cooker.

Brett Favre, the Packers Hall of Fame quarterback worked the clock and frantically drove the Packers offense downfield to the red zone inside the 20 yard line. They were at the 18 but time and hope were running out. It was fourth down with the clock stopped at only 4 seconds. A first down would do them no good, the clock would run out and the game would be over. They needed a touchdown on this play. Last chance. One play. It was do or die!

Brett Favre takes the snap and almost gets crushed from immediate penetration but he frantically spins away from a sure sack. Minnesota put on a ferocious rush and a sack would have been 'Game Over'. Right then the play they had called was now scratched and it was a sandlot football free for all. He looks right. Pumps. Nothing. Being chased he runs back to his left. Time has run out. Zero time on the clock. He's still scrambling, looking, trying to buy time for someone to get open. He backpedals under pressure then spins to his left and drills a pass into a crowd in the end zone..... Caught! TOUCHDOWN! GAME OVER! PACKERS WIN! The crowd went absolutely nuts and a frenzy like I've never seen before lasted for a solid 20 minutes or more!

It was party time at the tailgates in the parking lot!

That was the game experience of a lifetime. The entire experience was completely AD HOC and improvised each step of the way with nothing planned or arranged in advance. It came to fruition for no other reason than this PT willed it to happen and with his freedom, mobility and lust for life.

These are the types of situations and life experiences a free and mobile PT can create for himself.

The only way I could have possibly enjoyed this 'homeless' lifestyle was due to the fact that I had an internet based business which I could manage from the luxury of my mobile office. These days nearly every park or campsite has WiFi. It's a standard service.

I was fortunate enough to be able to buy the RV to begin with which was a blessing from heaven. But after that I really had no money and needed to be able to support myself which I did from my laptop in some of the most beautiful places in the world.

I'll never forget standing at the pump of a gas station fueling up. I was around 40 years old at the time. Another patron, an older man looked at me and then he looked at my rig with the Jeep in tow and said: "Hey! Aren't you too young to be retired?" I replied, "Yes, I'm not retired,. I just live like I am!"

This is one way of 'Living Free as a PT' and you can't beat it!

3

HOW I BECAME A 'PRIVATE TRAVELER'

This term 'Private Traveller' has legal significance. Many, perhaps you too, are waking up to what this really means. As I began studying the law in my days in Denver in the 90's it hit me like a brick that the law relating to the driver license, auto registration and regulations for 'drivers' applied only to 'commercial drivers' and did/do not apply to natural people who are not 'driving' for hire (commercial).

When you drive your family out for a picnic or to church are you engaged in commercial activity? Of course not. You are, by legal definition not a 'driver'. You are a traveller. A traveller moves about on the roads and highways as a matter of 'Right' under natural law and not by a regulated 'privilege' granted by the state. This is not the time or place for me to be giving a technical training on the legal aspects of that. I have that for you in other resources if you need it. Check the Appendix for references.

Previously herein I had mentioned that my time in the gulag was one of the best experiences I've ever had. One of the reasons for that was that it gave me time to do a thorough analysis and comparison of Man's law vs. God's law and this was incredibly enlightening.

You'll find 11 pages of quotes from biblical scripture in the appendix of ONE FREEMANS WAR which tell us in clear an unequivocal terms that we are to separate from the worldly

Babylonian systems and not be seeking those benefits which entrap us into that jurisdiction.

So with that as a backdrop, I began loosing those chains that bound me to the statutory world of subject citizens, drivers, residents, etc. I no longer wanted to be recognized as a resident, citizen, driver, etc.

The first thing I did was to get alternate documents and have my paid for car registered with the Embassy of Heaven church. The Embassy of Heaven takes the concept of 'separation of church and state' literally and why not? Either it 'is' or it 'isn't' a valid concept. I got my passport, ID/travel document, registration and indemnity certificate (aka insurance). Nobody could say I didn't have these things and they are 100% legitimate. Public officials can check to verify the documents and registrations directly with the church and it's done online.

The next thing I did was to take a hard look at the Certificate of Title to my car which was originally issued by the state. Knowing that the law clearly identifies this 'certificate' as 'title insurance' I decided I didn't want this title insurance anymore. Secondly, by registering the car with the state, the state held the true title which is the Manufacturers Statement of Origin (MSO) and it was the real owner.

On the certificate of title it says 'VOID IF ALTERED' on the front. On the back it said something like DO NOT MUTILATE.

So I took a bold black magic marker and wrote diagonally across the front in big bold letters: VOID.

Across the back I did the same thing and wrote CANCELLED.

I thought, that should be pretty clear. Sufficiently mutilated!

Now, based on my study of the law I understood very well that the 'registration' of any auto could only be done by someone who 'resided in' or was 'doing business in' THE STATE. This was clear.

The now voided certificate of title was sent to DMV with a cover letter indicating that this title insurance was now effectively cancelled and the DMV needed to make all necessary adjustments in their databases. I also requested the return of the MSO.

Secondly, I composed a letter to the Oklahoma Tax Commission which was the ultimate authority over registrations. It's funny how it has nothing to do with public safety but only taxes, right? Do you believe in coincidences?.

This letter was well crafted to seek confirmation of what I already knew but I wanted it in writing from the Tax Commission should the issue ever arise (in court) in the future.

I knew that it would be impossible to register a vehicle unless one were a 'resident' or 'doing business' in the state so my letter addressed these issues.

I had actually put my car into a trust which was the owner and now had the registration done with the Embassy of Heaven. Now that the car was registered to the church, to paraphrase, my letter went something like this;

======

Dear sirs,

I am writing to you today to seek the appropriate process for registering a vehicle. I have been having a difficult time and I need your direction.

This vehicle is used for non-commercial purposes of the Embassy of Heaven church which is neither a resident nor is engaged in any business in THE STATE OF OKLAHOMA. However, its use is primarily within the geographic boundaries of Oklahoma state and it is located and used in this area for the most part.

I wish to register it as local law enforcement will surely be asking when given the opportunity.

Please instruct me on how to properly register a non-commercial automobile whose owner is neither resident in nor doing business in THE STATE OF OKLAHOMA.

Thank you very much for your assistance and prompt reply to my address listed below.

======

I got the reply I was looking for which was basically: 'Sorry, you can't register this vehicle, you don't qualify.'

Perfect! I have tried to comply with the law in good faith and they wouldn't let me. The law cannot require the impossible. Should I ever have any issues about my 'non-state' 'Embassy of Heaven' plates and documents, I have an Ace up my sleeve and a 'Get Out of Jail Free' card.

I would need it.

My apartment at the time was in the heart of OKC and was right in between the City Police department on one side and a couple blocks to the other side was the county Sheriff Dept. So every time I drove home from somewhere, city police or Sheriffs deputy vehicles were swirling around me and would often stop behind me at traffic lights. With my Embassy of Heaven plates I remember always praying: "Lord make us invisible, make us invisible!" And he did. We never had any incident about the plates. Although I did take the precaution to buy a smoke colored plastic cover to put over the plates so they were a little less conspicuous. I never had any trouble.

One night while sleeping in the early morning hours in the OKC apartment my wife was startled and sat up abruptly. "What was that?" I was uninterested and wanted to sleep. She continued. "Mark, someone just closed the front door!" She was serious. Damn. I had to get up. We had a revolver in the room and I got it and started looking and listening. Nothing. I quickly looked around and noticed that the door was unlocked which it shouldn't have been and the curtains in front of the living room window where flapping in the breeze. The window was open. I quickly put 2 and 2 together and ran out the front door looking for whoever had just left. I ran out in my underwear, ran down the stairs into the parking lot to see the taillights of my Embassy of Heaven church registered car speeding down the road. There was no way for me to give chase. It was gone. I called the police at 2 AM. They were two blocks away and I thought there might be a good chance that their patrols on the street would see the car and get it. It took them 45 minutes to arrive to take the report from two blocks away in the middle of the night.

I went back into the house to do further inspection. We had just been to the bank that day and a packet of $2000 in cash was gone as was valuable jewelry my wife had stashed in a very obscure spot in the closet. We also found a cold half can of soda on the counter which the thief apparently took from the fridge and didn't have time to finish. The audacity!

A couple days after the heist we took off on another trip in the RV and left the recovery of the vehicle in the hands of the police. They had the full report. Off we went on our trip. I was in Kissime Florida talking to my mom on the phone telling her a little about our trip. I told here I was in Kissime. She and her husband had just returned home to Colorado from a golfing tournament they attended there and she said, 'Oh you're in Kissimie? We just came back from there and stayed at a beautiful park resort", and she went on to describe it and rave about it. As she went on describing it and how wonderful it was, I asked her, "Was it the Tropical Palms RV resort? Because that's where I am now!" She screamed, "Yes that's it! You're there now?" Ha! Amazing. It's a small world.

Anyway, we had a private mail service collect our mail back in OKC and every so often we'd have them pack it up and send it to us wherever we were. We were enjoying a wonderful time in Florida and we received our mail package.

In the package was a letter from an apartment complex in OKC which I had never heard of. The letter was to say that they found our car abandoned in their parking lot and found our mailing address on a paper in the glove box. They were charging us storage fees which were mounting up and if we didn't come pick it up and pay the storage within just a few days, they'd sell the car at auction as abandoned.

I thought to myself, 'Oh no you don't'. But what do we do? I told my wife that the police had the stolen vehicle report. We'll have them go pick it up and deal with it when we got back home. I mean, they need to be good for something don't they?

In the meantime, we had a date in St. Petersburg to see David-Wynn:Miller and attend one of his seminars where I was able to spend some time with him, pick his brain and share some stories. A good PT is always learning as he enjoys life.

Ace Up My Sleeve

So another successful trip in the RV ends up back in OKC and we contact the police. "Yes, we have the car. It's in the city impound lot. You have to go there, pay the tow charge and recover the car." Great. Off we went.

When we got there, we were informed that one of the tires was missing and there were no plates on the car and we find in the database that its' not registered. Interestingly enough it seemed that the thief liked our plates enough to steal them for himself.

Well that was good news anyway that my letter to cancel the 'title insurance' actually worked to cancel the registration. Now the problem was that law requires that for any car to be released from the city lot it needs to be registered to the state. Hmmm. What now?

I went to the city lot with some paperwork and tried to convince him to release the car. The fees were paid. It was my car, who is to say that some car registered in any other state or authority can't be released ? That's crazy. It makes no sense. The clerk wasn't moved. " It's the law. It has to be registered." He wasn't going to get into trouble for me that's for sure.

I made a couple of other visits hoping to find another clerk there and perhaps have better luck. It was always the same guy and he was getting tired of me.

Then, I remembered the letter I had from the Oklahoma Tax Commission. I don't know why I didn't think of this before! Duh!

So I dug it out of my files and came back again. He took a long look at it. I explained it was owned by a church (OKC is bible belt for sure) and he went to make a copy of the letter to cover his ass and get a second opinion. By virtue of this letter he was able to defer responsibility to a higher authority and pass the buck as they say.

He gave me the keys. I fixed the tire and got my car back! The state had succumbed to my maneuverings in the truth and law!

From this time on I was a sworn and true PRIVATE TRAVELLER traveling by right with no need for a license nor any corporate STATE car registration!

Fun with Registrations

While I was in Denver I had a good and growing group of patriots who regularly attended a weekly Law Club meeting I put on there and we'd always be discussing new research, ideas, and what we could do to push the envelope with those ideas.

On the topic of automobile registrations one of our friends told the story of having to pull over on the highway once to fix a flat. He hadn't cancelled his registration like I did but instead transferred the vehicle to a private trust and registered it that way to get his name off of the registration.

He was working on his flat roadside and a police cruiser pulled up behind him. Rather than offering to help, he started grilling our friend Curt with probing questions which were entirely inappropriate. Curt replied, 'Officer can't you see that I'm fixing a flat? There will be no 'fishing expeditions here today, thank you! The cop persisted demanding to see his paperwork perhaps hoping to dig up a little more revenue for his scoresheet before heading home for the day.

Curt got the flat fixed and went for his registration and insurance and nothing more. He had the car registered in the name of a trust. The trust name was listed as 'C.I.A. Trust' The cop tried to confirm, 'So you're with the CIA?'

Of course that could mean many things but Curt was smart enough to answer the question with a question and he replied, 'What does it say there?" And he shut up waiting for the cops reaction. His reaction was to give Curt the papers back and head back to his cruiser saying, "OK. I don't need anything more. Have a good night!

With that experience we started seeing a flurry of new vehicle registrations to trusts with names such as;

- Independence Research Services dba I.R.S.

- Financial Barometer Indexes, dba F.B.I.

And more. You get the idea.

See the appendix to learn how to have more fun on this issue.

Education is the key to unlock the golden door of freedom.
                - George Washington Carver

4
HOW I BECAME A 'PERMANENT TOURIST'

An important element in becoming a PT is the 'Permanent Tourist' aspect. This is basically positioning yourself so that wherever you are you appear as though you are from somewhere else. We discussed this previously. It doesn't mean you have to live on the road. It doesn't really mean that you even have to travel much at all if you prefer not to. Once you've gotten yourself positioned properly with the right documents you can stay or go wherever you want to be.

Pura Vida Mai!

This is a saying in Costa Rica which is culturally iconic and it basically means - Life is good man! Pura Vida! The pure life! I had visited Costa Rica on personal business a couple of times and fell in love with the country. My wife at the time had some business contacts there and I developed a few more and just before Y2k was about to possibly hit us. Everyone was debating the potential consequences.

We decided that we'd be much better off in the shade under a mango tree than in an RV which needs lots of gas, surrounded by snow and ice. So we sold the motorhome, took a big hit on the sale and prepared for the next adventure.

The day we sold the motor home was very sad. I remember the day the guy came to pick it up. When he drove it away, my wife cried tears and I felt the same. It felt like losing a very dear old friend.   Such great memories.   What a wonderful chapter in our life, closing.

The good news was that we were about to start a new life of adventure and exploration in Costa Rica. It was about as simple as buying an airline ticket and just skedaddling! We had nothing arranged in Costa Rica other than a hotel reservation. A mover packed our furniture and personal belongings and had them shipped in a container which would take about a month to 5 weeks to arrive. tWhere? We didn't know exactly. If I were to do it again, I'd just sell everything and start fresh in the new place.

So we arrived in San Jose and lived in a hotel for about 3 weeks with our Yorkie until we found a spectacular home to rent in a jungle on a mountain top. It was located at the end of the weaving road in a secure, exotic private development with a panoramic view looking down over the valley below. It was heaven.

I could write a book on my Costa Rica experience and maybe someday I will, but not here.

As for my status as a Permanent Tourist, I arrived with my American Passport but had no 'State' issued drivers license. Imagine that! I had previously cut it in half like an old credit card and returned it to the Colorado DMV with a nice letter basically saying…

…"Badges? Badges? We don't need no Stinkin' Badges!" Remember the old Clint Eastwood movie? Ha!

Anyway, you get the point.

So now being in Costa Rica, I wanted to have a Costa Rica DL. Had I had a valid DL from the US or any other place, I could have merely exchanged the foreign license for a Costa Rica license and be done with it. However, that not being the case, I'd have to take the written test and driving test before applying. So I did.

At the exam center they were nice enough to ask me if I'd like to take the written exam in English. I accepted. They distributed the local Spanish version to everyone else and I had to wait for the English version. And I waited. And I waited and after about 15 minutes had passed they finally brought me my exam. I whizzed through in about 8 minutes and was the first one out of the room. The others taking the exam looked like they were struggling with it. Anyway, that was quick. So I sailed through the requirements and got my Costa Rica DL.

While I lived there for 7 years, I hosted a number of business conferences and would routinely have a number of visitors wanting to get their own CR DL for obvious reasons. I'd have my assistant take the visitors down to the DMV center, get their required medical questionnaire and vision test completed and they'd be back in a couple of hours with their new DL! It was quick and easy.

Here's how this works to your benefit.

I was visiting family back in the states. I had a rental car and I'd be cruising through an area at a reasonable safe speed, which of course was speeding. I got pulled over. That NEVER happens, right? What are the odds?

So we start the routine with the officer. I give him the papers of the rental car (not registered to me), those papers show the insurance, and I give him my Costa Rica drivers license.

Immediately Mr. Officer is thinking to himself, "Hmmmm. It's not his car, he's not registered to the state, he's not a resident or doing business in the state, my state has no interstate compact with Costa Rica as we do other states in the US... no contract equals no jurisdiction equals no violation!

"OK Mr Emery. I pulled you over because you were going a little bit fast. Would you please slow down next time you're in the area? We'd like to see you have a safe and enjoyable visit. You're free to go. Have a nice time!"

I'm thinking to myself, now isn't that nice. I sure wish they treated me that way all the time! Well, maybe as a PT, from now on they will!

On the flip side, I got pulled over in Panama once. There, they don't chase you down in cars, they stand on the side of the road and point at you and you're suppose to pull over. It'a kind of like the IRS 'voluntary compliance' thing.

I've been 'pointed at' more than once in Panama and I'm like.... "Whaaa? Who? Where? Over there? And I keep going. I usually just ignore them. I'm just a dumb gringo! Who'd a thunk it?

The one time I did feel reasonably culpable to stop, you'll never guess what I did! I did what any reasonable Permanent Tourist would do, I pulled out my 'foreign' USA passport. He gave it a cursory look and not a word was said. He motioned me to go.

I did get pulled over in Panama city once for 'who knows what'? It didn't matter really. The poor tired, underpaid traffic cop made a deal. No ticket, 'if you just drive me home!' It's just a few blocks from here! He just wanted a ride!!

And in the developing countries there is no ticket that $10 can't fix. The routine is just like this, 'I'd like to pay the fine now and be done with it. What is it? $10? OK here. Be sure to pay it for me, OK?"

The people are so underpaid here that $10 or $20 holds some sway. It's not a bribe at all. You're pleading guilty and just asking the officer to pay the fine for you! They're honest, right? What could be done in more good faith and legal compliance than that?

The Permanent Tourist Residency Program

While living in Costa Rica for seven years I bought a couple of cars and paid cash, started several businesses, had two offices at one point for two difference businesses, I had personal bank accounts, several business bank accounts, a couple of different corporate attorneys, bought some land and lived in a gorgeous mountaintop home. One could say I was quite well entrenched in Costa Rica just like you'd expect of an 'old timer' who had a long history and family roots there.

I spent the entire time there on a 'tourist visa' which expires after 90 days.

At the time it was so simple. Tourists with the stamp on their passport could only legally stay in the country for 90 days before their 'tourist visa' expired. But to get another 90 day visa to be legal in the country, all you'd have to do is to leave the country and get an exit stamp on your passport, be gone for at least 3 days and when you'd come back you'd get a new 90 day tourist visa.

This onerous, heavy handed law forced me to take a series of long weekends and travel to explore the area. Can you imagine the horror?

The bus trip north to Granada Nicaragua was quite an experience. I stayed in the historic central district with my wife at the time and will never forget the little kids who had basically nothing, trying to hustle a quarter at a time shining shoes or doing whatever they could. Hardly any of them had shoes and I wondered how they managed walking on the hot pavement which was baking in the sun all day.

My wife agreed to take them all to the market and buy them some 'filp-flops'. It was so funny. When the appointed time came she met about 12 of them in the square and as she led them to the market it was like the Pied Piper of Hamilton. They all followed her calmly and practically in single file. You've never seen kids so happy as to have a $2.00 pair of sandals! They acted like they were in heaven!

It's amazing how such a little thing can make someone happy and it's the same with us. Remember that the next time you have a chance to be kind to someone.

During my stay in Granada a weekend fair was going on in the old colonial square in front of our hotel. We agreed to buy some of the kids meals as it was plenty of good food for a very low price and we could tell, they had nothing. I'll never forget some of these kids who'd receive a nice box of good food and many of them wouldn't eat it all. I thought that was odd. We finally asked them... why don't you eat?

"Oh I have to take some home to my mother, or brother because they don't have anything." It brought tears to our eyes. These kids who had nothing for themselves were so thoughtful for others they loved. What could we all learn from this?

On another weekend jaunt, I was 'forced' to hop on a small plane for the 45 minute light plane flight to the small Caribbean island of San Andres. San Andres is just off the coast of Costa Rica but is Colombian territory. It is well known as a tourist attraction largely for Johnny Cay, a small island in a series of 'keys' off of San Andres and it's known for its sugary white sand beaches and aquamarine shallow waters which make it perfect for swimming, snorkeling and other water sports. After suffering here for a few days we'd return back 'home' with our new 'PT Visa'.

Panama was a frequent destination as was Miami Beach where I got to know South Beach, Hollywood Beach and that area quite well.

So, you can see that to maintain my Permanent Tourist Visa status required diligence and commitment! In fact, this situation allowed me to maintain status as both: a 'Permanent Tourist' living as a permanent resident in Costa Rica and as a 'Perpetual Traveler' both at the same time.

I felt like I was starting to get good at this 'PT' stuff!

Society can overlook murder, adultery or swindling; it never forgives preaching of a new gospel.
                      - Edmund Burke

5

HOW I BECAME A 'PERSON OF TALENT'

Probably the single most important requirement of becoming a successful PT is in having the right mindset. You have got to be crystal clear in your own mind on who you are, where your power comes from, what you have to offer this world and be confident that your will and intent are so strong that nothing will stop you.

You get blocked, you go around the obstacle. You get stymied, you outsmart your opponent. No challenge will defeat you in achieving your goals. You must understand that at the beginning of your PT Quest, you'll have more questions than answers, but you move forward anyway.

You'll 'learn by doing' and along the way you're likely to rack up a pretty impressive string of experiences some of which will be failures which are nothing more than empowering building blocks of knowledge to get you closer to your goal despite the result. Throughout this process, you'll be developing the talents that you already have, and you'll be acquiring new ones.

Sadly, most people today don't have what it takes. They're too conditioned to be comfortable having someone else make their decisions for them and taking care of them. They wrap their personal identity up in 'what they do'. "Oh I'm an IT tech," or "Oh I'm a real estate professional", or "Oh, I'm a medical technician", etc. etc. etc. And that's how we define ourselves. That's 'who we are' and we live in that little limited world day and night and we die that way.

We get the pay that comes with the job, and no more. We get the respect that the community gives us for that 'job' and we accept that just fine. We get the feeling of security knowing that we have a paycheck to keep us from foreclosure for another month. And we don't have to have the responsibility of making the wrong decision too often because our boss, our company, our creditors, our bankers, our local town council and state and federal representatives are making most of the other decisions for us so we know who we have to pay, for what, and how much and how often and the decision is easy because if we don't…… it gets ugly.

I've seen comments on my YouTube channel saying things like, "I wish I had his confidence!'

Confidence is not something that can be given to you, nor can it be bought. It must be earned and acquired by the willful 'action' of pro-active people who are determined to succeed.

I'll give you the three keys to acquiring supreme, unshakeable confidence if you think you could use them. Most people won't, but I'll take the chance that you might. But before I do, let me give you an example of what you can do with this unshakeable supreme confidence.

I was looking at a piece of property in Panama. It was the most stunning gorgeous piece of property you could imagine. Imagine this. 19 Hectares (over 45 acres) of pristine tropical cloud forest with lush tropical vegetation and wildlife on the ridge of a mountain with views looking down on the skyline of Panama City and the Pacific coastline below. It backed up to the border of the Chagres National Park which is a forest preserve protected for its value as a water shed resource for the canal, so it would never be touched. It was perfect for the project I had in mind which was an eco-friendly natural spa and healing center for recovering patients. The air was pure and it felt ionized, it was perfect.

So I had to have it. But there was a small problem. The problem was that the property cost about $500,000 and I had only $50,000 cash and no credit. Through my passion and determination I was able to convince the seller to sell it to me on a short term contract. I would pay him $50,000 cash now to secure the contract and he'd give me 90 days to come up with the rest.

At the time I had no way, nor any idea on how to come up with the rest.

Now conventional thinking tells us what? It tells us that I'm an absolute fool for risking my last dollar with $49,999 others and making a commitment which, by all practical means and purposes I was highly likely to default on. What kind of a fool puts $50k at risk knowing he can't complete the commitment?

I'll tell you what kind of a fool. The kind of fool who is bound and determined to do whatever it takes to make it happen and who refuses to fail regardless of how many times the devil will tempt him to quit. This leads directly to the mindset we talked about above.

Losers will typically say: "Well I'll try." "I'll see what happens" and there is no commitment in that whatsoever. When you hear that, run because you're dealing with a loser. The person doesn't have the mindset to win, period.

So what did I do? First of all I prayed on it. I asked God for guidance on making the right decision and I prayed for assistance in making this a successful project to the glory of

HIS name. This is my silent partner and let me tell you, He's good!

I made the commitment, signed the contract, paid the $50k, and got busy. I started talking to consultants, realtors, money brokers, working out presentations to put together an investor group or a syndicate and I was talking to anybody who would listen. I found all kinds of talkers but few who could back it up and actually perform.

30 days came around and I needed to pay another $100k. I didn't have it. I only had $25k raised. I went and had a meeting with the seller. I showed him all that I was doing and what I had put into motion and sold him on my commitment to make this happen and that he'd get his money. He worked with me. We went through this routine with several deadlines coming and going and I fell short every time but was working my tail off to make it happen. The seller could see that and when the final deadline arrived to complete the contract, I had to renegotiate it and we agreed that I would pay extra interest for the delays. No problem. This property was worth it. The contract was still alive and so was my $50k!

In the end, I was way behind schedule having defaulted several times but I had finally accomplished what conventional wisdom would have told me I was crazy to even attempt by putting that $50k at risk to begin with. I had been stressed out many a night lying in bed thinking about what a fool I'd been to have paid all that money and now staring at a likely failure by all practical measures.

Through the grace of my partner (God himself) he softened the heart of the seller for me and worked with me enough to allow me to finally complete the contract.

Remember I told you that I only made that important decision after praying on it and waiting for the spirit to move me. Well, it turned out that the seller was also a Christian and was a fair minded, good hearted person which I didn't know in the beginning.

There are so many people out there who are only motivated by avarice and who would have been delighted to take my deposit and several significant payments as 'free money' when I defaulted on the contract, but it didn't happen that way.

So this is one of many examples I could use to illustrate how commitment, action and confidence are bonded into success with faith and the proper mindset.

So now, with this example as a backdrop, let's get back to the three keys in developing ultimate confidence. Here they are:

1. Turn off the TV and other distractions which waste your time and start reading and learning and empowering yourself with something new and productive every day. Days quickly turn into years and before you know it, you have years of acquired knowledge internalized.
2. Take this knowledge and apply it in practical ways in your life. There is no better teacher on this planet than experience. Be prepared to fail and expect it as a necessary requirement to learn and advance. Most people will use it as an excuse to quit. This is the difference between losers and winners.
3. Your biggest dreams, visions and plans are nothing compared to what God can do for you. HIS plan and love for you is so much greater than we can even imagine it's impossible for me to even try to describe. Your ability to make decisions and take action in faith, always seeking HIS counsel guidance and provision is a guaranteed formula for success even though sometimes

it doesn't appear that way initially. And we have to be careful how we define success. Success isn't always in getting what you want, but in getting what you need to be stronger, better, or better equipped to advance to the next level of personal and spiritual development! This doesn't mean that your plan or desires will arrive by limo all gift wrapped for you. You can expect to struggle, to stumble, to be exhausted to endure pain in getting to your goal but these things are the result of 'Action' done in 'Faith' with a willingness to sacrifice and do your part.

So with the foregoing in mind, to be a successful PT you will learn to be a Person of Talent, perhaps you'll discover talents you didn't even know you had or of talents you don't have now but will need to acquire or develop.

It's funny that on this big property deal I did, I had absolutely zero experience in real estate. None! Nada. I had only just purchased my first home in Panama at the age of about 48.

I had never done anything in real estate before either personally or professionally. I knew nothing about it and here I was wheeling and dealing in a land deal, leading to a multi-million dollar project in a country where I didn't hardly speak the language, it had a different legal system I wasn't familiar with so you get the idea. (This is where you can insert… 'WTF'?)

Now with the land deal under my belt, I was now working on the health resort project doing topographical mapping, project layout and design work, taking soil samples, doing environmental impact studies, doing water table analysis, getting necessary approvals and the works. Well, it wasn't me actually, of course it was my team but I was driving the stage coach with the reigns in one hand and the whip in the other.

So how do you do it if you have no experience? This is so simple. If you don't have the expertise, just build a team around you who does! Stay involved so you know what's going on. You learn as you go and after your first deal, you're all of a sudden the expert with first hand experience! You now have become a real 'Person of Talent' when you never had any of that talent before!

The key is taking action and you can do that without being 100% prepared or confident when you know you can rely on your silent partner to back you up!

Retired or Semi-Retired

Maybe you're fortunate enough to have sufficient fixed income coming in from investments or a passive business interest. You are in the perfect spot to be a PT. You can now spend more time developing your map of 5 flags.

Then you have the opportunity to develop your talents in things you have a passion for. Maybe you'd like to learn a new language or learn the fine art of perfecting French cuisine. Or if you love children you could coach a soccer team at the local school. In Central America you don't need to be certified. Just show up and volunteer and you're in!

Maybe you've always had a hankering to learn to play the guitar or harmonica! Harmonica is the best instrument to play and anyone can learn. Learn some blues licks and you can stick it in your pocket and take it to the beach, to a picnic, on a hike. anywhere you go. Try doing that with a piano!

Consultant or Self Employed

To be a successful PT you must have a source of cash flow to support your lifestyle, right? That's one of the obvious keys. And if you're not yet a seasoned entrepreneur you might be a little hesitant on this point.

Take heart. When you eliminate most of your debt and tax obligations (the Lighthouse Law Club can help you with that) your cost of living goes down dramatically and you'll be able to get by on much less than you are now. I can show you how to do that in another venue.

You've likely heard that when deciding on a business venture to start, you should find something that you have a passion for!

Maybe you're a health nut and you could start a nutritional coaching business.

Maybe you love music and you used to play in a band. You could set up an internet based exchange where musicians can offer custom songwriting, commercial licks and jingles and you sell a membership to the musicians to use your exchange.

If you have sales experience there is never a shortage of opportunities in that field and with the internet, affiliate marketing is huge! Go look for products you can promote at **clickbank.com** as one of many sources. Amazon even has an affiliate program. What market niche do you have a passion for?

Based on what your passion is, all you need to do is **'Find a need and fill it'.** And there is your business idea!

You can do some research and find out who is doing something successful in your niche. Find out what they are doing, add your own twist to their proven formula for success, add some new elements to it and make *their* success, *your new core business* only you are going to do it better!

I did exactly that back in the states. I was an independent credit repair consultant for a short time in the states and learned the ropes from an existing company I represented which did a good job.

I learned what I could from them and decided to do it myself. I went down to the local office supply story and bought a Do-It-Yourself credit repair forms kit for $10 and modified the letters and instructions to make them my own and of course I improved them. Then I put together a nice little assortment of low cost or no cost benefits and had all of the benefits printed up into a little booklet of coupons and I had my own company: The National Consumer Advocates.

I started selling this benefit package which was contained in a printed booklet. I could take a box of them and head to the nearest trade show or business gathering or public square event and make money wherever I wanted to go!

I started advertising and marketing the memberships and did fairly well with a borrowed idea, some improvements on it, some creativity and added value and I offered something people needed and benefited from. All of this starting from a $10 generic forms kit!

I Just Lit the Fuse and Ran Like Hell!

When I left the states for good, I had my sights set on Costa Rica as mentioned earlier. I basically packed up, got a one-way ticket and took off with no plan whatsoever. I knew what I wanted (out of the corral!) I had a certain amount of cash in savings which would last me maybe 5 or 6 months but that was it!

I had no existing business to generate income. I had no plan or special contacts to help me out. The internet was in its infancy and was nothing compared to what it is now.

I made up my mind that I was leaving and headed to Costa Rica and that was my plan of action. Period.

I'd have to figure what to do from there later on and did so starting from scratch. So I landed in San Jose, got a hotel room, started exploring and I put on my thinking cap with radar turned up to high sensitivity!

I had to figure out how to support myself, my wife and a cute little dog and the fuse was lit. I had about 5 months before my money ran out and the bomb went off.

I had to ask myself, what was my passion? Freedom and Personal Privacy

What was my experience? International living, travel and business in general with some newly acquired skills and knowledge on trusts, trust management and asset protection.

What was a need that people had which needed to be filled? The problem was that Big Brother was spying on everyone and ruining peoples' lives on a whim whenever they wanted to because they had total control.

That was it! I'd create a membership club which people could join to learn how to live a private life and protect themselves from intrusion or worse. Privacy Club International was born and started growing.

It was created about 3 months into the 5 month fuse and by the time my fuse was burned up, thankfully the bomb never exploded. It was defused as I was then toddling in my new business and it grew from there. I did it with plenty of help and thanks to my silent partner of course!

Key Point Summary: Some people need to have everything in perfect order before they make a move. This is wrong thinking.

Why? Two reasons. Because;

A)   Nothing is ever in perfect order. If it is, something changes bringing it all to chaos. And this person then never accomplishes anything because nothing is ever in perfect order for long, if ever, and they never take action as a result. A person of talent knows precisely where he's going and the result he's seeking it's just that the road to get there may not be discovered yet but he's moving anyway. He is able to think on the fly, make adjustments find the right path if not create a new one which never existed before and then adapt to his conditions to make it work for him knowing that he'll find the way in the end.

B)   This same person in A) is relying entirely on himself to make the perfect plan which is a very poor choice. You've seen how I step forward taking action and making 'crazy' commitments I shouldn't make and yet somehow being successful. Is it because I have the Midas touch? Hardly. If I had to rely entirely on myself and my abilities I'd be scared to death. It's because I have the security and comfort with ultimate faith in my 'silent partner'. He's always got my back!

This gives me comfort and confidence to dive head first into this crazy world and expect nothing but the best results, even though there may be a price. Nothing is gained without a price. Nothing is valued without a price.

6

HOW I BECAME A 'PREVIOUS TAXPAYER'

For some odd reason this topic seems to hold a lot of interest to a big segment of the more 'productive' population of the western world.

For a time I was reasonably successful selling health insurance for a large insurance company. One year I earned a very nice little bonus. I worked hard to achieve that and made a lot of sacrifices along the way to get it.

I was a city guy out selling insurance to the farmers and ranchers in Colorado. I'd be out on the lonely county roads busting through snow drifts or wallowing through mud holes in my 'no clearance' jet black Firebird TransAm (I loved that car). On more than one occasion I needed to find a truck or tractor to extricate me from a jam. That poor car!

So when I filed my taxes that year (back when I was young and foolish) the IRS came back and wanted a more than healthy share of my bonus. I said, 'Sorry! You didn't work for it, I did!'

That started me on the path of seeking knowledge and truth and I started studying the law with the help of some groups who specialized in that area. Once I learned the truth in 1990, I have never filed another 1040 in my life. Why? Because I don't have to! It's pretty simple.

Legal Tax Avoidance

An investor with a substantial income from his stocks and bonds who is from from Canada would normally be obliged to pay almost half of his earnings to the Canadian government. He could choose to reduce his tax burden in the most common, but ill-advised way, which is to hire a tax accountant to explore all the loopholes, allowances, deductions, deferments and tax free exchanges. But this is ill advised.

It's expensive first of all. Secondly, when push comes to shove your accountant works for the state and not you. Loyalty? Think again. Thirdly, one mistake and you are in tax accounting hell if not jail! These are not attractive options.

Tax violations are only civil violations in many countries. But Canada, the UK and the United States have made tax evasion into a criminal offense, resulting in what are in effect, 'debtors prisons' for those who don't tow the line and who don't know any better. It would be far more sensible for this Canadian investor to break free and become a PT.

By merely moving abroad and establishing a legally recognized residence and domicile in a 'tax friendly country', this Canadian investor would be able to legally avoid handing over half of his income to the bureau-rats. He would then also be free to roam the world as he desired, provided he did not remain anywhere outside of his new tax friendly home long enough to be considered resident there for tax purposes.

Thus, the PT legally avoids all income taxes without resorting to fraud, because it is not necessary. A PT who is properly situated need never file tax returns, government required disclosure forms or any other paperwork.

What do I mean when I say 'tax friendly country'? This would be any country which does not tax its people on 'foreign earned income'. Panama is currently one example of many countries which are like this. If your money is earned out of the country and stays out of the country, it's tax free as far as they are concerned! Most of the world operates this way. It's called a 'territorial tax system'.

Countries with "territorial" tax systems only tax residents on income earned within the borders of the country. Foreign earned income and foreign-source investment income is generally not taxed. Just to name a few countries with territorial tax systems would include: Costa Rica, Hong Kong, Panama, Seychelles, Singapore, Taiwan.

Some countries have no personal income tax at all. (They rely on consumption taxes, import tariffs, property taxes, etc, although some do have payroll taxes on domestic salaries). An incomplete list of countries with no general income tax include: Andorra, Anguilla, Bahamas, Bermuda, British Virgin Islands, Cayman Islands, Monaco, Nevis, Turks and Caicos Islands, United Arab Emirates, Vanuatu.

Bad news for U.S. Citizens...You are taxed no matter where your income comes from! If you get a job as a Sherpa in Mongolia and you don't report the Mongolian tögrög which you earned, you are technically a criminal. The U.S. passport is deemed the most expensive passport in the world to have for just this reason alone.

But have no worries if you hold that expensive USA passport. Keeping the IRS at arms length is as easy at taking candy from a baby (although I would never suggest to take candy from a baby!)

The IRS mafia collections racket is a system of distraint based on fraudulent inducement to volunteer. This is perpetuated by the willful ignorance of its victims which is created in a climate of fear and intimidation to cover up the 'bluff'.

This is not the time or place to get into details on this but if this subject interests you, you definitely need to read volume #2 in the ONE FREEMANS WAR book series:

HOW I BEAT SATAN...AND THE IRS!

It's a quick, easy and fun read and it doesn't get bogged down in eye glazing legal technical analysis. Get it if you want quick hard facts which you can verify for yourself. For perhaps the first time ever you will see the fraud as clear as day!

If you ever have dreams of being a 'Previous Taxpayer' you have to start thinking for yourself and with a little bit of study your tax accountant will be paying 'you' for lessons!

WARNING: If you're going to put your life in the hands of your attorney and accountant to do your thinking for you, this isn't going to work for you. You need to think for yourself. You need to understand that as well intentioned good people as these professional types might be, they are trained by 'the corporate farm managers' to keep the cattle in the barnyard and producing milk! I don't think I need to explain that.

So let's wrap this section up with some key questions people ask and you can explore the answers on your own to trigger your own thought process.

Q: So Mark, are you saying you don't pay your taxes?
A: Hell no I'm not saying that! I pay a lot of taxes. I pay taxes on nearly every thing I do, nearly every transaction I make. I just don't file any 1040 form and I surely don't pay any income taxes.

Q: Why not?
A: Simple. Because I'm not required to. I'm not a 'Taxpayer' by definition.

Q: How do you manage that?
A: Simple. I don't have any 'income'. If someone doesn't have any reportable 'income' they're not a 'Taxpayer' and are not required to file.

Q: So if you have no income, how do you live?
A: Let's start by understanding the legal definition of 'income' I make sure that I don't have income. However, I do get compensated for my services and I do have access to resources and cash flow for various purposes. Again, the law is very specific: cash flow is not necessarily 'income' by legal definition and the courts have supported this time and again. Most people have no idea what 'income' really is. Again, I follow the law.

Q: So how do you achieve that?
A: It's very simple and there are many ways to do it. The key is to learn to 'Live like a King while being a Pauper on Paper'. This is what we teach to members at the Lighthouse Law Club.

Q: Aren't you afraid of getting into trouble?
A: If I were afraid of getting into trouble do you think I'd be writing books, doing videos, speaking in public international conferences and teaching the law to as many people as I can possibly reach? I'm a student of the law. I follow the law. I teach others to follow the law and learn it well enough to be free forever!

I have positioned myself as a 'Previous Taxpayer' so that I can enrich the world with 100% of the talent, skills, invention, creativity and all the blessings God has given me.

This allows me to pay cash for my cars, and travel as I like. I have no debt and move about freely. I keep what I make and I share it with the needy.

So who is morally correct here? Someone like me who contributes his energy to the world in a positive way? Or someone who dutifully 'pays his fair share' to war hawks, liars, thieves and baby killers who wish to enslave him?

Think about it.

Need I say more?

"The art of taxation consists in so plucking the goose as to obtain the largest possible amount of feathers with the smallest possible amount of hissing."

- Jean Baptiste Colbert

7

HOW I BECAME 'PREPARED THOROUGHLY'

I'm a gun lover. I love guns not only for the obvious benefits and uses for self defense but for recreational use also. My dad was an avid hunter and I've been handling guns since I was 7 years old.

As a kid I always had 'BB' guns and pellet guns and have been plinking tin cans since I can remember. I learned to handle a .22 pistol at an early age and since we were hunters I had my own 20 gauge pump shotgun since I was 10. My dad and I had our own clay pigeon thrower and would spend hours trying to knock them out of the sky in pieces. At one point I was getting pretty good at it.

I'll never forget the shot of a lifetime my dad made. We lived in the country for a time and had a lot of bats flying around at dusk in summertime. Just for fun, he took out a .22 pistol to see what he could do and damn, if he didn't nail one with a pistol shot and knock it dead out of the air. That's a nearly impossible shot. It's difficult enough to hit a standing target with a pistol but a bat darting around like a fly at dusk? Wow!

So, fast forward and I'm now living in my new home in Costa Rica. At the time I had a collection of guns which were still back in the states.

I had a couple of M1-A1 .30 caliber (7.62 mm) carbines which I loved. I had the 'Paratrooper' version which is a lightweight, easy to use semi-automatic rifle which was a standard for the U.S. military during World War II, the Korean War and well into the Vietnam War.

With those I also had a Chinese made SKS. The SKS was originally a Soviet semi-automatic carbine chambered for the same 7.62 x 39 round. The SKS is popular on the civilian surplus market as a hunting and marksmanship semi-automatic rifle. Its simplicity, durability and accuracy made it popular and it was relatively inexpensive to purchase. It used steel cased 7.62×39mm ammunition which is one of the least expensive center fire cartridges available. I picked mine up at a gun show for not much more than $100 and later bought another one just for the value.

I'll never forget taking my first shot on the target range with it. It packed a serious punch!

With my little 'babies' of course I had a collection of 20 and 30 round banana clips to complement the carbines which were all interchangeable. Along the way I had acquired some 'novelty items' such as tracer rounds, armor piercing rounds and some fun stuff like that.

So here we are now having made the move to Costa Rica and I had to ask myself the question, "What am I going to do with my guns?" I did some investigation with customs and the airlines and found out that all I needed to do was to put them in a locked case, mark the case, declare them appropriately and there'd be no problem bringing them in to Costa Rica by commercial airline. So that was the plan.

My wife at the time, was planning a singular visit back to Oklahoma to visit family and she agreed to manage it for me while she was there. Great! I was all set.

As part of the preparation and packing process she was trying to remove the cartridges which were loaded in the banana clips. However, the springs in the clips were quite strong and this process was hurting her fingers. So she stopped emptying the clips thinking that she'd have her son finish the job for her later.

She got everything packed up ready for the trip back to Costa Rica. The rifles were locked in their cases and declared to the airline at check-in. She took the clips in her carry-on luggage.

It wasn't until she was seated in mid-flight when she broke out into a cold sweat! She had just remembered that she never finished removing the cartridges from the clips and she was on board an international flight with a half dozen 20 and 30 round banana clips fully loaded and some with armor piercing military rounds! (This was around the year 2000 before 9/11 and TSA).

So she arrives at San Jose International airport fearful for what might happen to her, she picks up the rifles and reluctantly heads toward the customs checkpoint. By nothing short of a miracle, nobody was manning the luggage scanner so she just walked right through customs fully armed and loaded with enough armament to hold off a SWAT team!

When she got past the checkpoint without issue, she practically melted in disbelief and relief!

Upon arriving home, she was so happy not to be in prison and I was so happy to have my 'babies'.

It wasn't long before I had a need for one of them.

We lived on a mountain top in the last house at the end of the road surrounded by a jungle in an exclusive development. Neighbors were near enough but none were in sight. The nearest ones were down the road a bit.

I had a 55 gallon barrel I wanted to use to burn trash in. But it wouldn't burn without air flow and it needed some holes in the bottom to let air in to fuel the fires I wanted to burn. I tried punching holes but the metal was too heavy gauge for that to work. So I went and got one of my rifles. What better use for my amor piercing rounds? I wasn't expecting any tanks to be coming up the hill anytime soon, especially since Costa Rica doesn't even have a military.

So I got everything set up properly with the empty barrel up against a hill for a backdrop so there would be no errant bullets and I started shooting. It was LOUD. The sound reverberated through the mountain rainforest.

I was the new guy in the neighborhood and I can only imagine what people must have been thinking who were not too far off. Finally, one of the neighbors called to see what was going on and if everything was alright.

I explained and told her not to worry, but she didn't quite understand. I heard later through the grapevine that the word going around was that 'I was trying to start a fire with my rifle." That surely must have made quite an impact on the neighbors as they tried to evaluate what kind of lunatic they had on their hands now.

In any event, I made myself known and with my amor piercing rounds and M1 carbines I was 'Prepared Thoroughly' for the job at hand and any other which might come later! I don't think anyone around had any thoughts of messing with me!

8

BUSINESS & BANKING FOR 'PROPER TRADE'

Back in the good old days when tax havens were operating out in the open with global acceptance, the world was a fanciful place to be a freewheeling privacy seeker and you could set yourself up and move around with ease and freedom. That was a very nice world to live in.

However, things have changed quite a bit since then. The '94 'deep state', staged bomb attack of the Alfred P. Murrah federal building in Oklahoma City* triggered some long standing 'anti-terrorist' (read that, 'anti-privacy') legislation which was previously getting nowhere. This was one of the first dominos to fall in the war on privacy. For more on this see 'One Freemans War…'

Remember Teddy Roosevelt's famous words:

> *"In politics there is always a reason for circumstances to exist."*

Without getting deep into the weeds on that discussion suffice it to say that since then, there has been a concerted attack on freedom and privacy worldwide.

The 9/11 demolition of the World Trade Center in 2001 triggered 'The Patriot Act' which, by no accident, was largely written before the WTC towers were professionally demolished under the guise of 'foreign sponsored terrorism'. The Patriot Act, contrary to what the title might infer, targets 'Patriots' as it ushered in the new and improved surveillance state which gutted privacy rights all in favor of 'security' from 'terrorists'.

The sad, or funny thing is, depending on how you look at it, is that the Act was promulgated under the guise of protecting the people *'from'* terrorists, when the fact of the matter is, that the government now has the means to protect itself *'from' the people* whom they consider are the 'real terrorists'!

As it turns out, in the effort to drain the swamp the deep state does have quite a bit to be concerned about as it relates to 'the people' as they are currently being exposed, de-funded and de-fanged by a joint and elaborate multi-national effort from populist forces around the globe.

The OECD, (Organization of Economic Cooperation & Development) has continually applied legal, political and economic pressure on the so-called 'tax haven' countries to fall in line with this globalist effort. The objective has been to get the 'tax havens' to give up the ghost and start sharing information and charging 'fair' taxes. 'Fair' in this context is considered to be whatever high taxes the European or OECD countries charge, so they can't be undercut by the competition which is working much more efficiently and attracting significant capital away from the slave ships of the 'modern industrial world' i.e. G-8 and OECD.

FATCA

To ensure that information on its wandering freedom seeking prisoners could be 'shared' and 'fair taxes' could be imposed, the US did it's part by enacting FATCA which is the Financial Account & Tax Compliance Act which basically makes all banks globally an unpaid administrator for the

IRS, whereby they spy and report on all Americans who have any accounts overseas.

FATCA requires all foreign banks to collect the Social Security number, passport, local address and more on their American clients along with other tax information and have the client sign various IRS disclosure forms when filling out the foreign bank account applications. Then, the foreign bank is required to store this data and make periodic reports back to the IRS on their American clients.

'Balderdash' you say! How does the IRS have the jurisdiction, or how does US Congress have the authority to make foreign entities bow to them?

They don't. But here's how they do it: They basically say to all banks around the world, "Hey banker! If you still intend to use the US dollar and use US correspondent intermediary banks for your bank wires, (which they all do for the most part) here's what we require you to do: you will be our unpaid agent, collect the information, do our admin work for us, send us reports on our prisoners 'er taxpayers on a regular basis and if you don't, we'll retain 30% of all the money you pass through our correspondent banks. Deal?

The foreign banks have only two choices; 1 - submit to the tyranny and start reporting their American clients, or 2 - just stop dealing with American clients altogether. Sadly, this is the option chosen for many institutions. Americans and their business are simply no longer welcome.

Either way, it's bad for Americans.

FBAR

If The Patriot Act and FATCA were not enough of an insult to it's own people, enter stage left the Foreign Bank Accounts Reporting requirement. The FBAR requires:

> "Taxpayers with an interest in, or signature or other authority over, foreign financial accounts whose aggregate value exceeded $10,000 at any time ... generally must **file**."

So US Citizens' banks abroad are reporting them as a result of legislative chicanery. FBAR now requires that US Citizens give up their privacy and 5th Amendment rights to be secure in their papers, personal effects and property. And if they don't 'self violate' those rights voluntarily, they consider US Citizens to be criminals and will act accordingly.

Perhaps now you're starting to see how the US passport is known as the most expensive passport in the world to hold. Perhaps you might even be seeing how it is more than that. It has become a serious liability for anyone who wants to be free in this world.

SARs

U.S. banks are now required to file 'Suspicious Activity Reports' on any transaction which involves $3000 or more in cash. If you withdraw $3500 cash to buy a used car, or anything it doesn't matter what, you are being reported to FINCEN (Financial Crimes Enforcement Network).

Cash is now deemed 'suspicious' and in many cases can be seized on a whim by law enforcement without any criminal charges ever being made. It's a joke and 'free money' for the police. I'm not going into that here but be sure you inform yourself and do a search for 'Civil Asset Forfeiture' and read a few articles to know what is going on.

CTRs

A currency transaction report (CTR) is a report that U.S. financial institutions are required to file with FinCEN for each deposit, withdrawal, exchange of currency, or other payment or transfer, by, through, or to the financial institution which involves a transaction in currency of more than $10,000.

So in today's world;
- Any transaction over $10,000 is reported to FINCEN
- Any cash transaction of $3,000 or more is deemed suspicious and is reported to FINCEN
- Any foreign account opening for US passport holders is reported to the IRS via FATCA.

The New CRS

And with all of this the OECD was not satisfied. As of January 1, 2017 over 100 countries signed on to the 'Common Reporting Standards' which essentially is a global FATCA for other non-U.S. countries. Financial institutions will now give you a CRS form to complete to declare your tax residency. In other words, where you are required to pay your taxes. Your personal and account information will be sent by the financial institution to the tax authorities of the country of your 'tax residency' so that you cannot escape scrutiny and the blood hounds will be on to your 'scent'.

But don't worry. It's all folly and intended to entrap the ignorant zombies of the world. Critical thinkers and smart entrepreneurs can easily render such efforts to have no impact whatsoever. There are ways to drop off the radar and avoid all of this which we'll explore a little further on.

Offshore Companies and Banking

It used to be a simple matter of setting up an offshore company and bank account and that alone would provide sufficient privacy to manage your life and business without interference or molestation.

Not too long ago you could appoint (and still can to a lesser degree) nominee directors provided by the law firm you are using or you can come up with your own.

It was also common that many jurisdictions gladly offered 'Bearer Shares' so that the owner of the company was 'whoever' had the shares in their possession.

This isn't done much anymore thanks to the strangulation efforts of the OECD and their offensive against privacy and low taxes. Let's face it, the globalists don't want anyone to be free and independent. They want everyone under surveillance and in their control. That's the war we wage through no choice of our own.

These days the banks live in fear of the regulators and are happy to chase you and your business away simply to 'stay safe' with the regulators whom they are in bed with. They never say 'no we don't want your business'. What they do is give you a list of requirements and when you complete that list, they give you another one and they just keep asking for more documentation and more requirements to the point of absurdity until you just say 'F*ck this!' and you give up the account opening process altogether as being completely ridiculous and excessively onerous.

Dealing with the banks has become extremely frustrating to say the least. And with U.S. regulations, many foreign banks now are not even interested in dealing with clients who carry that 'evil' passport.

The above notwithstanding, in applying for a corporate bank account one must be prepared. This means having a clear picture of the purpose and expected activity that the company will have.

The bank will want to know things like:
- What is the business activity of the company?
- Who are the clients?
- Where do the clients come from? Which country?
- Are they consumers or other companies?
- What is the average transaction size?
- How many transactions might you expect in a month?
- How many and how much in total deposits per month?
- How many and how much in total withdrawals per month?

In other words, you'll need to present the bank with a pretty complete corporate profile and then have your activity conform fairly closely to that profile. Sudden aberrations without notice could be cause for concern by the bank and put your account in question.

Once the account is opened, many banks are now requiring to see the invoices involved in supporting the underlying transactions for wire transfers in and out. They want to see supporting documentation underlying the transactions.

So the days of just opening an account and sending or receiving funds willy nilly are pretty much over.

Is Your Business Politically Correct?

If the above were not enough to discourage you before you even started, consider that payment platforms and many banks are requiring also that your business be politically correct before they entertain your business. Or even if you'd had years of stellar performance as a client, it can be decided overnight that your business is no longer welcome at the bank.

We have seen that companies which are 'deemed' to be non-compliant with the globalist agenda have had their accounts shut down for no valid reason if any reason at all.

Just recently we've seen PayPal shut down the account of Alex Jones and **infowars.com**. Across the board many gun manufacturers have had their accounts closed or denied simply due to the nature of the legal business they are in. Do a search for 'gun manufacturers bank accounts closed' and read up on it.

Christians are 'High Risk'

You might be aware that I started a humanitarian foundation in Panama to help the needy and spread the good news of the gospel along the way. It's called The Panama Christian Foundation or 'PCF'.

We were denied bank accounts by several banks simply because they viewed 'Christian' organizations as a 'high risk' venture. We had a solid business model much more viable than the usual ministry begging for donations.

With the trouble we went through I swear we could have gotten accounts set up in the blink of an eye had our business model been gambling or porn. Those are 'main stream businesses' with high turnover. Christian missions, not so much. The bankers weren't interested. Or, could we chalk it up to the globalists starting to put the squeeze on Christians and marginalizing us? We know that's a part of the long term plan. I don't know. You be the judge.

Banks are 'De-Risking'

Here's an excerpt from an interesting article on this subject from The Guardian:

"How would you feel if you were dumped by your bank with no explanation?

You've been a loyal customer for years, but then a letter arrives saying your bank has decided it will shut your accounts, and you will have to take your business elsewhere. No reason is given and the decision is final.

Guardian Money can reveal that the numbers of people being given the boot by their bank appear to have increased sharply. And Samuel (he didn't want us to use his full name) is the latest person to be on the receiving end of this Kafkaesque treatment. Like many of those affected by this, he believes he is a victim of discrimination.

Samuel, a father of two preschool-age children who lives in Kent, contacted Money after NatWest told him he was being dumped. He's been with the bank for more than 10 years, but it wrote to him on 12 January to say that it had, "with regret", decided it would be closing his four personal accounts, plus the joint account he shares with his wife. The couple also have a NatWest mortgage, and the bank is "strongly recommending" that they give serious thought to moving it to another lender.

Samuel has been given 60 days to find a bank willing to take him on, though NatWest told him: "We will not be able to provide references for you." In the meantime he must cut up and return his debit card.

So what, some will wonder, has Samuel done to merit being treated like a pariah? He told us he can't think of any reason why the 71% taxpayer-owned bank is so keen to be shot of him, and says he and his family have been treated like "criminals".

With the bank refusing to say anything about Samuel's case, it's hard to avoid concluding that NatWest, and some other banks, are dumping customers and organizations with links to countries about which they have concerns.

Samuel was born in Nigeria and moved to the UK more than a decade ago. His full name is unmistakably of African origin, though he hasn't been back to Nigeria for more than eight years. Notably, NatWest is now closing the accounts held solely by Samuel's wife, who was born in mainland Europe. Both have permanent residence cards from the Home Office.

In March 2015, Money reported how economics professor Iraj Hashi had had his NatWest current account, savings accounts and credit card shut down with no explanation The only reason he could think of was that he was born in Iran.

Last April the Guardian related how a UK law firm was handling more than 60 companies by Iranian nationals who had had their UK accounts closed. Meanwhile the Guardian's sister paper the Observer last year reported on the case of Mohammad Rahman, who had his bank accounts frozen and then closed by Barclays.

You can perhaps see a theme here: many of those affected are of Asian or African origin. So what's going on? Welcome to the secretive world of bank "de-risking".

———-

I had the same thing happen to a U.S. bank account held by an LLC I set set up there. There were several years of solid activity and never a problem of any kind.

Without notice or inquiry they sent me a letter saying that according to their account agreement they can close the account anytime for any or no reason and they offered none. They just said, 'you have 30 days to clear out the account and wrap things up. See ya!'

I was using a debit card drawing on the account and those transactions were typically for charges and ATMs in Panama. I could only figure, 'De-Risking'.

'Yes Go Ahead'!

While living and doing business in Costa Rica I had a scam artist try to get me to send him money and he'd guarantee it with a check which he instructed me to hold for 'collateral'. The check was for $100,000 and was drawn on an international bank against the account of Chevron in Lagos Nigeria. Chevron of course is a big international oil company, one of many which are very actively doing big business in the oil rich OPEC country of Nigeria. The scamster was from Nigeria. The 'advance' he wanted was much less than the amount of the check but still a nice amount for 'free money'.

He made it look attractive but his request made absolutely no business sense whatsoever and bells were going off everywhere of course.

Naturally wary, I called my banker to send a representative to my office to review the check with me in person and discuss the matter.

There was no way I would try to deposit this without their pre-approval. I was not going to jeopardize my account for some flim-flam man and stupid greed. I certainly knew better than that.

So the girl from the bank comes over. My first cause for concern was about the bank itself and not the check. Her reaction when she saw the check in the amount of $100,000 was, 'Ohh, that's too much!' I was like, 'What?' What do you mean 'too much'? This is a business check for business purposes, from Chevron (supposedly)." I was thinking, 'so you are an international bank catering to business and you've never seen a check for $100,000?' I was taken aback by that, but this is the state of banking these days. People you expect to be professional and know their job, 'aren't and don't!

So we get over that and discuss it further. I told her point blank, "I will not deposit this if there is any doubt or hesitation by the bank or if it comes back as a bad check to have consequences against me and my account.

She assured me that in no way would I be held responsible if the check were not good. If it didn't clear, it would simply be returned without consequence and that would be that.

"You're sure? You're absolutely sure and you promise me that your supervisor agrees?" We called the supervisor and she agreed.

So I reluctantly deposited the check and they processed it. It was fraudulent and they immediately closed my account without discussion.

De-Risking (and lying) at the customers expense!

Lesson learned. Unless you're dealing with the bank president or highly experienced and seasoned V.P. don't ever trust anything ever told to you by 'supervisors' or 'managers' as they are generally low level clerks with absolutely no business experience or street savvy whatsoever.

I cannot tell you how many times I've had to instruct clients how to train their own local bank personnel on how to properly initiate a simple international bank wire transfer. Most people working in the U.S. banks below the V.P. level simply have no clue whatsoever on much of anything. You pretty much need to tell them how to do their job. Be warned.

Banks Dealing with Foreigners

As a part of this De-Risking process where most international banks were previously standing with their arms open to welcome the business from foreigners in years past, they are now changing their tune.

When I started getting to know Panama, around the turn of the century (that sounds so old, doesn't it?) it was a banking, tax and privacy haven *'par excellence'*. Being the crossroads of the world and a global commercial and financial center due to the canal, shipping, trans-shipping, a global logistics center etc. foreigners were flying in, getting their business and banking set up and flying out again and it was almost like the banks had revolving doors which were spinning constantly. "Sign here, give us a copy of your passport make a deposit and get out of here, next!" Those were the days.

I remember when there were upwards of 180 international banks registered in Panama. Banks like UBS, Duetcshe Bank, Citibank and all the big names with plenty of smaller banks making a run for the money as well. It was a banking and financial haven. In contrast there might be only 45 today with banking mergers, acquisitions and market shakeout.

Beyond Panama I've opened business accounts in Hong Kong, Sweden, St. Kitts, British Virgin Islands, Belize, Costa Rica, The Republic of Georgia, Chile and various other jurisdictions. Most of those I didn't even step foot in the country. It was all done online and documents sent by courier. Typically, you set up a company in that country and through your registered agent for the company you establish a local registered address and then through whatever your official capacity might be you set up the company account and start doing business.

The Ultimate PT Bank Account Opening

I remember attending a financial conference in Chile in 2012. I was an American passport holder, a Panama resident, visiting Chile as a tourist and I was able to sit with a representative of a bank in the Republic of Georgia where I opened an account for my business in Hong Kong and it was as though I were ordering a new phone service. Fill this out, sign here, send a couple things next week, and you'll have your account! Cool! And this was not so long ago.

There are still places you can do it this way, but the more prominent jurisdictions are shunning that old type of business and favoring local businesses run by local residents and in any event, a personal visit is required.

I had one favorite bank in Panama and had a great relationship there for several years. I knew the bank manager personally and we met frequently so we knew each other well. One day the bank just decided they didn't want clients with American passports anymore and they shut me down without so much as a 'Thank You'. This was around the time that FATCA was approved. I couldn't believe it.

So now that you are thoroughly convinced that offshore banking may not be for you, let's shift gears and discuss some solutions and ways to 'work around' some of these issues.

Proxies and Nominees

When searching for a legal service provider to help you set up your corporate, banking and other legal affairs be sure to ask them about 'Nominee Directors' and if they provide that service. Typically nominee directors are used to seed the corporate board of directors and their names would appear (not yours) on the formation documents and hence the public registry.

It's not very common that a nominee director would be used to set up the bank account but it is a possibility to discuss. First of all they don't know you or how you'll handle your business and they don't want any liability for what idiot clients might do since banking and finance is a sensitive issue. Secondly, you don't know them and they are typically mid to lower level employees of the legal firm and they may not have the proper professional profile to best represent your business or handle your banking and if their employment terminates with the firm, you'd need to pay legal fees to appoint a new director and update the registry. But still, it might be something to discuss and explore.

I have known cases where the client has a good and long standing relationship with an attorney or other trusted professional and that person is appointed perhaps with a limited power of attorney to set up and/or manage the banking function which keeps the client 'off the books' per se.

Most all of the normal banking functions can be done by the person with the internet access codes and if that person is you or the designated 'person in charge', then you don't have much to worry about with the nominees since they don't have that access. They are there in name only in the formation documents and for the public registry and little more.

Checks and Balances for the Nominee Directors

One way to protect against possible malfeasance by nominees is to have them tender signed but undated resignation letters. With these in hand, any unsavory act which might occur can be rendered as being 'without authority' and thus criminal by you dating the resignation letter appropriately and putting them on notice. This could get someone into some pretty hot water under the right circumstances and is a good insurance policy although you'd likely never need it.

With many years of experience and having dealt with many firms in various countries, I've never heard of this ever being necessary. It's more of a psychological crutch than a necessity which is ever used. But, just as you hopefully have never used the guardrails on a curvy mountain road, they still serve an important role.

Power of Attorney

It's typical that when using nominees who are locals in the jurisdiction of registry that they serve their role for privacy purposes only and generally have no other role or activity in the company unless you've appointed them to have a role.

They can sign a corporate resolution from time to time and this is coordinated by your contact in the law firm anyway so they generally don't know anything about the company nor are involved in any way. That's your job!

The directors would typically pass a resolution and then issue a General Power of Attorney giving you full authority for anywhere from 1 to 3 years to do any act on their behalf to provide company management. You then become the 'attorney in fact' and can run the company. The POA is a private document in most cases although it can be put in the public registry if needed for business purposes.

It would then be entirely appropriate for you to sign your name with the title, 'Your Name - attorney'. Most people don't know the difference between 'attorney-at-law' and 'attorney-in-fact' and by merely seeing that you are listed as the 'attorney' for the company they rest on their own limited knowledge and make their own assumptions and presumptions. Your statement was correct. Run with it! You can usually get a wider berth operating that way, if you know what I mean.

Share Certificates

The company formation process requires the issuance of the share certificates to show beneficial ownership and this is clearly noted in the formation documents. Transparency is now a key word in everything including company ownership. Gone are the days when company ownership could be concealed with 'Bearer Shares' which belong to whoever holds the certificate that moment and there is no 'name' of record as the 'owner'. I remember those days and they were great.

However the OECD has made sufficient threats and done enough brow beating on the countries previously known as 'tax havens' so that having a company with 'Bearer Shares' is now considered taboo and is no longer done for the most part. Where it is still allowed there are restrictions and you can't get a bank account without putting the bearer shares in the custody or on deposit with either the bank or the attorney and have the owner of record on file.

One way to thumb your nose at the OECD is to use nominees on the board and have the share certificates issued to one or more of the board of director nominees.

He/they then would simply endorse the back of the share certificates gifting them to '_____' and the registered share certificate then becomes a 'bearer share' by virtue of a blank endorsement. It's just like endorsing a check made out to you, over to a third party.

In this case the share was not 'issued' as a bearer share so it's fully compliant, but circumstances surrounding the 'transfer' have subsequently converted it privately and legally. This only gets noted on the corporate books when you want it to be. In a closely held company they could be held in this state indefinitely. Just be careful to keep them safe.

Professional Trustees

This is one of the better options if you're seeking a local contact person with an address and with local personal and professional history to initiate and/or manage corporate finances and banking. Being registered and/or regulated and certainly licensed puts them at a high level of risk if they should do anything contrary to their mandate and/or the interests of the company and/or you.

The Ultimate Beneficial Owner

In view of today's requirements for 'transparency' one can no longer hide behind a company or any type of fictional legal entity. At some point the 'individual' behind the business must be identified and do KYC when dealing with banks or financial institutions.

For example in Panama, when dealing with a law firm to set up a Foundation of Private Interest, or an S.A. or any type of entity, law now requires that a form be filled out to properly identify the U.B.O. (ultimate beneficial owner) Thankfully, this does not go on the public record and can remain private from the public but the law firm must keep it on file privately and if there's ever an official investigation that information must be made available to appropriate authorities when requested.

Fair enough. We can manage that. It's a legal requirement which most privacy jurisdictions had no interest in to begin with but they implemented it to satisfy the OECD and stay off the 'grey lists'. It really has little practical meaning so long as you never invite a full legal investigation due to some nefarious activities and if your business activity and banking are set up in other jurisdictions there is very little any local authorities would be able to do in any event. You don't live in the same jurisdiction as the company, the banking is in a 3rd jurisdiction and the clients and business activity come from the 4th 5th and 6th jurisdictions. So for practical matters, it's a moot point.

So now you see how the five flag strategy is working for you in practical terms.

Setting Up a Global Network

Let's just say you have a company set up in Chile. Most of your clients and business comes from the USA. But you want to trade cryptocurrencies on a European platform which only accepts Euro and not USD.

You might be wise to have an LLC and bank account in the USA to receive local funds from customers there.

Your main holding account is in Chile so perhaps once or twice a month you sweep the USA LLC account and send those funds to Chile.

A portion of those funds you want to go to the trading account in Europe. Most Chile banks allow you to do business in Euro, USD or the Chilean peso. So your USD from the USA goes to Chile where it can be converted to Euro and sent to your European trading account.

Problem, many banks now are looking for invoices to document the purpose and legitimacy of the transfer and this gets to be a royal pain when it's your own money going from one corporate account to another.

Problem solved: One thought is to have all of these companies with the same or very similar name. When you transfer from one entity to another with the same or similar name, you can merely chalk it up as an 'internal corporate transfer', which it is and nobody bats an eye.

For example: The USA LLC does sales and sends funds to the parent or 'holding company' in Chile. The holding company has a subsidiary in Europe or the U.K. which is set up for 'asset management' and it does the trading. All are interconnected and serve a common business purpose while performing separate roles. Different branches to the same tree, if you will.

The issue you'll have to solve is the KYC requirements for each. Many financial institutions want to see that the principal can offer proof of residence, proper ID etc. etc. Ideally, there would be one person in each local jurisdiction whom you could call on for this role. Most institutions do not require the UBO to be a local resident so search this out when selecting your service providers but keep this in mind in your planning.

But with that being a common issue, we'll have a solution for that in the next chapter.

Just the Beginning

These are just a few ideas and some basic points to get you thinking. The list of possibilities and strategies is endless and limited only by your imagination. The beautiful thing about living as a PT in the international arena is that whatever obstacle you might be dealing with as a result of any BS anti-privacy legislation and the intended restrictions on your freedom and rights, there is always a way to defeat it and STAY FREE!

Remember….the politicians who pass these laws to control 'you' always leave an 'open back door' for themselves! Regulations are only for the idiots who can't think. Never forget that.

We have more to come. Keep reading!

The question isn't 'who is going to let me'; it is 'who is going to stop me?'

- Ayn Rand

9

THE MYSTICAL MAGICAL SUIT 'PREFERABLY TEFLON'

A recurring theme which I continually hit on in many of my teachings is that we must 'know who we are'. As simplistic and parochial as that may sound on the surface, it is actually a profound study which provides the fundamental basis from which all other thoughts, concepts, analyses and acts must emerge. Get this wrong, and everything else you do will be wrong or at least 'askew' when compared to your full potential.

This is a deep subject and in no way will I be able to properly address it here but let's at least touch on the surface and get you started in thinking about it.

Being 'dressed in a teflon suit' is a metaphor for the idea that 'nothing sticks to you'. To achieve this status you must understand the operation of law.

We've already discussed practical examples of how I've avoided;

- Traffic tickets - because I had no contract as a 'resident' or 'citizen'.
- Income taxes - because I have no income and am not a 'taxpayer' and thus not required to file.

This concept operates on multiple levels.

One level is such that we can ask 'who am I as it relates to the social compact and my legal status with 'a','b','c' government?'

Another level, among others, is when we ask ourselves, 'Who am I as it relates to my being here on this earth and what is the purpose and mission of my life?' Or said another way, 'What is the nature of my relationship (contract) to my creator?

As you can see, we're starting to deal with the issue of 'legal status'.

The bible recognizes this concept clearly in Matthew 17:25 when Jesus spoke:

"What do you think Simon? From whom do the kings of the earth take toll or tribute? From their sons or from others? Simon said, 'From others'. Jesus said to him, "Then the sons are free."

So we can say with confidence that 'legal status' is everything.

Back to the operation of law:

There is 'natural law' which is universal and endowed upon all of mankind by our creator. We all have an innate awareness that is built within us to know what personal human rights are. We don't need to go to school for that. We just know it inherently as it comes from our creator and is in our DNA and is reflected in our customs and culture which has been passed to us through the centuries. It is the inherent knowledge of right and wrong.

Then there is 'legislative code' which is created by governmental bodies (man). This 'code' always operates on the corporate level. Corporate governance only applies to the directors, shareholders, beneficiaries and others who are contracted to the corporation. Are you starting to see the picture?

People often complain to officials, in court or elsewhere, 'I have rights! You're violating my rights' Well, when you're dealing with the corporation, I'm sorry to tell you but 'No you don't' have rights. You are subject to the *contract* and you are in the jurisdiction of the corporation. The corporation does not recognize your natural law rights. It only recognizes the *terms of the contract*, mostly which are hidden and you don't even know about, so stop screaming for your rights when you don't even understand the nature of the venue which you are in.

In the USA it is clearly established law that each of the several states of the union are foreign corporations as they relate to the UNITED STATES federal government corporation which is exclusively the ten miles square of the District of Columbia, its territories, military bases, docks, arsenals and ceded enclaves. So if you were born in the District of Columbia, congratulations! You are a U.S. Citizen!

What? You weren't born in D.C. and you were born among the several states? Then how did you get to be a U.S. corporate citizen?

Here's how: You contracted to receive benefits from U.S. Inc. and in the process of applying for benefits, you had to admit or vow that you are a U.S. Citizen when in fact you weren't. It's called 'fraudulent inducement' based on 'lack of full disclosure'. They tricked you and sucked you in!

What benefits did you apply for?
- A job with the government or military
- Social Security

- FDIC insurance when you opened a bank account
- Government guaranteed loan of any kind.
- US Passport
- And so many others, just to name a few.

For our non-USA readers, I'll be using the USA as an example here but the concept applies to all nation states globally. The operation of law is the same. You have been converted from your state of natural law and God-given rights and blessings to one of 'corporate beneficiary and serf'.

Now, when we previously discussed the banking and finance legislation such as FATCA, FBAR and related intrusive legislation which all violate the natural person's right to privacy, who does that legislation apply to in the USA? Yep. U.S. Citizens!

So, with that understanding let's cut to the chase. People are learning about the fraud and it's being exposed. The best news is that a growing number of alert and awake freedom lovers are learning how to 'correct the record'.

Here's one example for illustration:

One man that I'm aware of has recently completed the process of correcting the record with the U.S. State Department, as it relates to his passport. This basically amounts to applying for a new passport to replace one previously issued in error (incorrect status) and rather than signing the application as a 'U.S. Citizen', he submits the application as a 'Texan', born and raised upon the land in the geographical boundaries of Texas state (not THE STATE OF TEXAS which is a fiction/corporation).

This is an American man (not 'person') who is native to one of the several states which is, by law, foreign to THE UNITED STATES corporation and thus he is not a U.S.

Citizen. With his application for the passport he includes a detailed 'Explanatory Statement' which is a memorandum of law which supports his position.

The Department of State accepts the application for passport on those (his) terms, they accept his fee and it now becomes a matter of contract and permanent record that this man is a 'Texan' and NOT a U.S. Citizen.

The man's application paperwork is 'the offer'. When the Department of State issues the passport based on the offer, they have 'accepted the offer'. The fees the man pays are the 'legal consideration' which supports what is now 'the contract'. THE UNITED STATES is now bound by contract to honor and respect this man's legal status and not impose obligations they would otherwise impose on their own U.S. Citizens.

This is confirmed by documentation he receives when he does a FOIA request (Freedom of Information Act) for his files on permanent record with the U.S. State Department. Do you see how beautiful it is to understand the operation of law and how it can work for you?

So this American state, non-U.S. citizen tries to open a foreign bank account with his U.S. passport. The bank does the usual and presents him with the FATCA paperwork to complete and sign which is required of all U.S. Citizens.

He shows the bank his State Department files confirming that he is in fact and in law a 'Texan-American' and NOT a U.S. Citizen and once the bank understands this properly they then happily allow him to proceed with his account opening process WITHOUT the FATCA paperwork.

Chalk up a victory to the successful, well informed PT!

For those who might be skeptical let me just say that the explanatory statement which accompanies the modified passport application is an 11 page legal memorandum.

Here are just 3 U.S. Federal Court citations used in that memorandum which might help clarify your thinking;

"A person who is a citizen of the United States (Federal government; Fourteenth Amendment citizen) is necessarily a citizen of the particular state in which he resides. But a person may be a citizen of a particular state and not a citizen of the United States (Federal government; Fourteenth Amendment citizen). To hold otherwise would be to deny to the state the highest exercise of its sovereignty, - the right to declare who are its citizens."
 - [State v. Fowler, 41 La. Ann. 380]
   [6 S. 602 (1889), emphasis added]

It is quite clear, then, that **there is a citizenship of the United States** *(Federal government; Fourteenth Amendment citizen)* **and a citizenship of a State**, *which are distinct from each other and which depend upon different characteristics or circumstances in the individual.*
 - [Slaughter House Cases, 83 U.S. 36] [(1873) emphasis added]

*"There is **a distinction between citizenship of the United States** (Federal government; Fourteenth Amendment citizen) **and citizenship of a particular state**, and a person may be the former without being the latter."*
- *[Alla v. Kornfeld, 84 F.Supp. 823]*

So now, in view of the above are you starting to think about arranging for your new Magical, Mystical Teflon Suit? Mine is pretty comfortable!

10

FREEDOM BEGINS WITH A 'PRIVATE TRUST'

Up to this point everything we've covered is almost meaningless if you don't have a rock solid financial fortress as a base of operation. This chapter deals with just such a piece which is critical on your strategic chessboard.

We've talked about your teflon suit, your legal status and positioning in the 5 flag strategy and related concepts. All that is quite important but if you don't have an exempt and impenetrable vehicle to receive, hold and build upon the fruits of your labor, your heritage, legacy and future estate, then it's all for naught.

This short chapter will not be a training on such subject matter but will introduce you to the key concepts with which you would be wise to continue your study and take the proper action to implement a plan using those concepts as your guide.

There are trusts. And there are 'trusts'. They sound the same. They look similar. They're spelled the same. But there is a world of difference.

One type is recognized, dealt with and treated in the statutory jurisprudence of most legal jurisdictions. It has specific legal characteristics and functions which make it just another form of legal creature created by, regulated and controlled by the corporate state government.

The other type has been a closely held secret used by the Super Rich to manage their wealth in such a way as to be literally untouchable and free from the constraints of regulation, taxation, intrusion, inspection, disclosure and/or legal processes.

The uninformed or 'institutionally educated' will scoff at that idea and deny even the possibility of such an animal existing so let me present an example of its existence and power for you, right up front.

Nelson Rockefeller served as the 41st Vice President of the United States from **1974** to 1977. The Senate Subcommittee investigating Nelson Rockefeller's financial disclosures before his approval as vice-presidential candidate notes for the record:

"Due to the complexity and <u>lack of legal means necessary</u> under law to secure in-depth records of the Rockefeller estate, <u>nor having the powers to abridge the right of contract</u>, we must assume that the $218,000,000 figure is accurate."
 - The Rockefeller File, Gary Allen, 1976

So ask yourself this: "How is it that the senate subcommittee would lack the legal means necessary to secure the in depth records of the Rockefeller estate to verify the information on his disclosure forms?"

And then further, "How would his privacy be protected by 'the right of contract' which the Senate subcommittee cannot abridge?"

The answer is simple. He was using one of the secret trusts used by the Super Rich (and The Lighthouse Law Club).

Why is it 'secret'? Because of course it's not taught in law school nor is it in practical use by the general public or anyone in the professional community aside from those very few 'in the know' and who 'have a need' internally for their very special clients. This information is not generally known 'on the street'. If it were, the legal profession would be in danger of extinction because people wouldn't need attorneys to untangle the mess of the statutory codes which complicate peoples' lives and which don't apply to these secret trusts.

Further, government revenues would dry up overnight if everyone were 'tax exempt' as this legal animal is.

You can see why it's a 'secret' and when others in the mainstream see such an animal they laugh, scoff, ridicule and will tell you that it's invalid and not worth the paper it's written on or worse, that you'll get into serious trouble for using one. Oh really? Since when did 'contracts' become 'illegal'? Nice try. Enough said.

I have copies of signed letters from the IRS stating, to paraphrase in part;

"Dear Taxpayer,
We cannot process your application for an Employer Identification Number. (These) trust organizations have no tax requirements therefore an E.I.N. is not required. ...."

And to further understand this important point, let me share with you an excerpt from 'TAX FREE HOW THE SUPER RICH DO IT' by Don L. Wood and First America Research:

— — — — — — — —-

"Periodic and always interesting lists of the so-called "Super Rich" frequently appear. Yet, when consulted for certain names, we find they are omitted or that the wealth reported is far less than believable. Who, then, are the truly Super Rich? They are the ones who are unimpressed by such lists.

Most if not all of their riches and property are privately held and not subject to discovery. They use a reclusive business vehicle affording complete privacy yet they enjoy absolute power to control their financial affairs.

The famed columnist, Jack Anderson, has some interesting insight on this subject: "We have had access to secret tax filings by members of our wealthiest families, the Mellons, the Rockefellers, the Hunts and others. Their returns have one thing in common. Each of the families has had millionaire members, who from time to time, have paid no income tax at all. And almost all of them regularly pay only a fraction of the tax their incomes would require were it not for loopholes.

Vice President Nelson Rockefeller, for example, paid no federal income tax in 1970. His brother, John D. Rockefeller III, pays a 10 per cent federal tax as a matter of personal principle. Apparently, he can manipulate his tax exemptions to produce whatever tax return he feels is appropriate. Paul Mellon, worth a cool one 'billion dollars, is able to get away with negligible income tax, as do other members of his fabulously rich family. And Texas oil millionaire Bunker Hunt has managed to live in luxury without paying any taxes at all in several years.

We do not single them out for criticism. They have made use of the law

— — — — — — — —

So imagine for a minute having your home, business, savings, investments, retirement and other important assets owned, not by you, but by a legal entity which was positioned so that legal predators, as the Senate subcommittee was quoted saying in Rockefeller's case, 'lacked the legal means necessary to secure in depth records…' or to snoop or find out anything about those assets whatsoever.

Imagine having your business and investments growing nicely without any tax liability. When you factor in the compounding effect of new found capital when anywhere from 15% to 35% or more is not being siphoned off the top every year, the difference is astronomical over time.

And please, don't even think of giving me the most ignorant and asinine comment, "Well that's not patriotic. Everyone must pay their fair share!" If you think this way then please, just stop reading this book right now and throw it in the trash because this is not for you!

While you're at it, do a quick internet search for '$21 Trillion missing'. Ask yourself how much did your family sacrifice as you contributed 'your fair share' to this stolen money? And we won't even bring up the long list of other morally objectionable expenditures that 'your fair share' supports.

If you want to play the morality card, OK then let's play it. When you know your tax dollars are supporting; illegal wars, black ops, the surveillance state, FEMA death camps, weaponized weather machines, baby killing factories, directed energy weapons, satanic education in the schools, toxic vaccines, graft, pet projects for the politicos, people who don't want to work, foreigners who enter illegally and expect you to pay for their apartments with big screen TVs, and the list goes on, you are voluntarily, knowingly and willfully complicit with evil. There is no way around it. So my question to you is, "Why do you knowingly support evil?"

I'll tell you what 'my fair share is': I work hard to make not so much for me and my family. I do 100% of the work and my fair share of that is 100% which benefits me, my family, my community and my pet projects. When I keep 100% of the fruits of my labor I have a little extra I can spread around to help others who really need it and where it can really have a positive impact on this world.

Government has so much hidden, stolen money, they don't even need to collect taxes. They do so only to continue the 'ruse' by perpetuating the premise that 'they need it to provide roads (and other B.S.) and cover up the fact that they've already stolen more than one can accurately count. Do some research on the C.A.F.R.s, (the Combined Annual Financial Reports) and that'll open your eyes.

So I'm going to keep my fair share of the fruits of my work and my fair share is 100%. You do what you want with yours. Support evil if you like but don't pull this 'morality' or 'patriotic duty' play on me because it doesn't fly.

So the key to wealth building and asset protection is so simple, I'll give it to you right here in one simple phrase:

Learn to be a Pauper on Paper, And Live Like a King!

So when they haul you into court by the scruff of your neck and throw you down onto the table in front of the judge and they force you to fill out a financial statement of personal net worth you can honestly list under penalty of perjury;

1. Used Computer — $ 500
2. A couple of dirty shirts. — $ 30
3. An old dog with vet bills — $?
4. A used pickup. — $1500
5. Checking account — $ 100

The 'Private Trust' is not 'yours' as you don't 'own it' and while it may have a nice round figure of assets under management with a decent cash flow, again, 'It's not yours'.

It is a separate legal entity and the judge *"does not have the legal means to secure in depth records..."* remember?
So being a pauper on paper has its advantages. And when public records reflect that you own nothing of value, how many predatory freeloaders with greedy attorneys do you think will want to sue you looking for a free meal ticket?

Got it? Simple enough.

Now, the fact that the Private Trust is able to provide you a palatial home and send you to 'business events' around the world and provide a nice company car and debit card for expenses as support for your services makes your lifestyle 'bearable' for a guy with a personal net worth of only around $2000. I think you are starting to see the picture.

I was in court in front of a judge once and she was trying to establish jurisdiction by asking me some questions to get me to admit I was a resident 'subject'.

It went like this.

Judge (J): "Where do you reside?"
Me   : "I don't have a permanent residence. I'm a sojourning pilgrim traveling throughout God's beautiful kingdom."

J.   : "So Mr. Mark where are you employed?
Me: I'm not employed. I'm not unemployed. I'm not employable. That's not what I do.

J: "So how do you live? How do you support yourself?"
Me: : "I live by the grace of God. Thank you for your concern. And you?

J.   : Bailiff please see Mr. Mark out. You are free to go!

I'm just a sojourning pauper. No permanent residence, no job, no ties. And for that reason most of the rest of the world has no interest in me! I trust that the above needs no further explanation.

Yes, I know you have a thousand questions. What about this? What about that? These are all things we can deal with in the Lighthouse Law Club. The list is far too lengthy to address here.

The subject of trusts, privacy and asset protection is a fascinating one. Volumes have been written and we have some of the most detailed, best researched, legally supported and hard to find treatises on the subject anywhere. Suffice it to say that it would be impossible to give the subject proper treatment here. But if this intrigues you, check the appendix for references to additional material you can start boning up on right away.

"Civilization is the progress toward a society of privacy. The savage's whole existence is public, ruled by the laws of his tribe. Civilization is the process of setting man free from men."

— Ayn Rand

11

THE ALT-BANK SOLUTION FOR 'PREEMINENT TRANSACTIONS'

So now we've already discussed many of the practical issues (problems) we have in dealing with banks. Let me take it a step further and say without reservation or equivocation: "The debt based modern banking and monetary systems are the greatest evil that this world faces. They are the direct cause of scarcity, poverty, war, strife and the subjugation of national sovereignty where national governments work against the interests of their own people." And if you don't agree, you have some homework to do.

The Big Picture

Whereas in the days of yore, when conquest required large armies and treasuries, these days the banking system is the new weapon being used to conquer entire nations. Armies are no longer needed. We can look to the practices of the IMF, the World Bank and the Central Banks around the world to see how debt is the new weapon of choice to subdue entire nations and their people.

Just for the record let me give you a current example to illustrate my point. The example is Greece. Here's some background from Wikipedia:

"Greece joined the European Communities (subsequently subsumed by the European Union) on 1 January 1981, ushering in a period of sustained growth. Widespread investments in industrial enterprises and heavy infrastructure, as well as funds from the European Union and growing revenues from tourism, shipping and a fast-growing service sector raised the country's standard of living to unprecedented levels. The country adopted the Euro in 2001 and over the next 7 years the country's GDP per capita more than doubled, from $13,070 in 2001 to $28,660 in 2008. The Greek government, encouraged by the European Commission, European Central Bank, private banking institutions, and the Greek business community also took out loans to pay Greek and foreign infrastructure companies for a wide variety of infrastructure projects such as those related to the 2004 Summer Olympic Games in Athens.

Government deficits were also consistently underreported. As the Financial crisis of 2007-08 began to affect Greece's economy, the country's GDP stagnated between 2008 to 2010 and the government's capacity to repay its creditors was drastically reduced."

So Greece (and most all other countries) was encouraged to take on loads of debt premised on the basis of a fast growing economy. This was the seduction. *'Things are good! Take the money!'*

Any student taking economics 101 will tell you that all economies go through cycles and the boom years don't last forever. The central bankers knew this. They took Econ 101 (most politicians haven't). So they loaded up Greece with debt which eventually they couldn't pay as soon as the cycle turned.

Faced with default they were forced to the negotiation (spanking) table with its creditors where they were forced to take a 'deal'. The deal went like this, "We'll bail you out of your current crisis with a new and/or re-structured debt, BUT you have to implement severe austerity measures which will hurt your people and further depress your economy (so we can get paid instead) AND you have to give us your infrastructure. We want your ports, electric and all energy production, transportation systems, hospitals, etc. etc. The bankers then control the country and profits which would otherwise be going into private industry and economic growth or even government coffers to help it's people or pay back debt is now being siphoned away from the people and into the bankers pockets.

It's then no surprise that Greece is now in a 'worse' situation and it's only a matter of time before the economy collapses under the debt. The bankers foreclose on 'everything' and have total control.

You see how this works? Using this method of national takeover, call it a 'soft coup' the European Central Bank, World Bank and IMF virtually control all of the developing countries and several of the developed ones.

Central Banks vs. National Banks

The same thing has already happened in the USA. Let me explain to help those who may be somehow unaware.

The founding fathers had intended for the USA to have a national treasury (controlled ultimately by the people) which would create and control the money supply (real money not 'debt notes'). The plan was for money to be created as an asset and ledgered and then 'spent' into circulation via public works projects and programs. This is a simplistic description but valid nonetheless.

After various failed attempts, the money powers of the world were able to establish a private and foreign 'central bank' in the USA which was untouchable and outside the confines and reach of the government. This central bank would then take over the nation through its vast influence and tentacles of monetary control.

Here's how that worked:

The Federal Reserve Bank does not 'spend' money into circulation. It is a debt based system and money is 'lent' into circulation with interest.

Consider the Fed as a private family business, which is what it is. So this family business can now 'print' as much of the debt based currency (federal reserve notes) as it desires, or even better, just create digits on the computer and 'lends' these electronic digits, or paper notes whereby the recipient needs to pay back **full face value PLUS interest**.

So let's say this is your business. Your family can print a $100 bill for 2.5 cents or $0.025. You lend it to your neighbor, who now has to pay you back $100 PLUS interest. If he doesn't pay you back, you take his house or whatever he owns. (get the concept, not the math)

Now here's the catch. You are pumping out $100 bills like crazy! This is a fantastic business with unheard of profits. The only fiat currency in circulation is the actual face value of the notes circulated. If everyone were to pay back their loan at once, where does the fiat currency to pay the interest come from? It doesn't because it doesn't exist. Only the face value of the notes in circulation exists. The only way for debtors to pay their loans back, is to borrow more debt. Remember Greece?

So what this means, in very simple terms, is that it is a mathematical **certainty** that a certain portion of the population MUST fail financially because there is not enough currency in circulation to pay all the debt on the books. So a fixed amount of financial failure is programmed into the system. Whatever happened to 'The Land of Opportunity?'

So meanwhile, in addition to the astronomical cash profits your family business has been making, you now start accumulating a lot of assets as you foreclose on the failed loans.

And because you have a nifty deal with the government of the United States where they borrow trillions from you, you need some collateral to back up all this debt, right?

So in order for the United States to be able to put up some collateral as in: 'the full faith and credit of the United States' they pull a trick on Americans who are state citizens and not yet US Citizens which by legal definition only includes the ten square miles of Washington D.C. and its territories, forts, docks and arsenals, as you know now.

They offer these Americans certain incentives and benefits to cross over to the new jurisdiction. To get those benefits, these Americans have to volunteer/admit/lie that they are US Citizens when they sign the application forms and without telling anybody about the trick, everyone thinks they're just a US Citizen and always have been, never really knowing the difference, the truth or knowing what is happening.

So now, without ever realizing it, your labor, your property, your family's future has become the property (collateral) to back up the 'full faith and credit of the United States'. When the private U.S. government corporation borrows trillions, wastes trillions and loses trillions of the money they got from the Fed family business they don't worry about paying it back because they have you, your labor and everything you own as collateral which gets them off the hook with the Fed.

Now when the entire system collapses and goes into default, and it's a mathematical certainty that it will, and probably sooner than later, guess who owns everything you ever worked for your entire life? Whoever it is, it's NOT YOU! How does that feel?

Now, this is programmed servitude and destruction. Can you honestly tell me that this is not evil?

So back to the family business: the family is now acquiring so much wealth it starts buying up the means of production, moving it overseas to make greater profits from slave labor and leaving millions of workers at home unemployed which increases foreclosures and the assets on the balance sheet. The economy dips and everyone suffers.

It starts buying up the media companies and forming media conglomerates which the family can now control to condition the masses to its way of thinking.

It starts buying up the banks, brokers, exchanges and financial services companies and it can now 'rig' the financial markets for favorable financial and political results. It can buy up shipping & transportation companies. Agricultural production can be consolidated into massive corporate farms putting the family farmer out of business and destroying personal independence.

The wealth can be spread around and used to influence what's being taught in schools and universities. It can be used to acquire the main producers in the pharmaceutical industry and with control of the media and medical associations that they have, they can push drugs on everyone to make them passive, detached and dependent.

And with this consolidated wealth and control, comes political influence where the family business can now control local, state and national legislative and judicial organs which can pass laws favoring the 'family business' and put any competitors or challengers 'out of business' by hook or by crook.

Since they make many billions from 'cancer research' projects and drugs, actual cancer cures are suppressed. The money is in the 'treatments' and not the cure. That's where the money is. If you start curing people they don't need to buy drugs and that's not the plan.

If the central bankers want to create a bubble in real estate or the stock market and inflate prices, they'll just flood the market with new money and with these easy money policies, people have money to spend from cheap credit and prices will go up and the family can rake in huge profits when they sell their holdings at the highest prices. They do this before they tighten monetary policy and crash the markets.

But still, with the crash they can collect more assets and just mop up from foreclosures and buy assets for pennies on the dollar. To do this they just raise the interest rates and tighten money supply to slow the economy and put additional financial stress on debtors. This accelerates defaults and they can then pick up millions of properties and other collateral which goes into default and thus they benefit immensely from the misery of others! Heads, we win! Tails, You lose!

And here we are. Welcome to today's globalism brought to you by the fine folks in the family business called THE FEDERAL RESERVE BANK and other central bankers near you!

So now you should fully understand my opening statement about the evils of the bankers, banking and the monetary system. You can learn more on this subject on the YouTube channel for the Lighthouse Law Club. I have an entire playlist entitled, RUN BANKERS RUN! Check it out.

So, what do we do about it? Read on.

The Solution

The solution couldn't be simpler. Pull out of the banking system and start using alternatives. Pull out of the tax collection system by re-asserting your original status as a natural born creature of God aka John-Millhouse: Doe and not the debtor of a cestui-que-vie trust, artificial entity, aka U.S. Citizen, aka JOHN DOE.

I trust that you likely understand what I just said, if not, don't get hung up on it. You'll learn soon enough if you follow the breadcrumbs. So what are the alternatives?

The alternative to using fiat currency which is a continually losing buying power as a 'depreciating' asset due to inflation and taxes is to start using 'appreciating' assets to hold, store and spend your value. If you get paid in fiat currency, immediately convert it to alternative assets which will at least hold their valued have a good chance to appreciate. These would be; precious metals, food production, useful capital equipment, low cost properties which can produce rental income and even a basket of value based crypto currencies. You get the idea.

For U.S. passport holders the alternative to being a U.S. Citizen is to learn to revert to your original status as an 'American' or state citizen or simply 'bug out' and find another more suitable passport to use. The same holds true for other nationalities.

The alternative to being under the thumb of the tax collectors is to;

a) Set the record straight using the law in your favor to establish your good faith and compliance with the law and stop the tax collectors in their tracks with their illegal activities. We do this routinely.

b) Quit your 'J.O.B.' and learn to profit from your own business. If that's not possible or desirable for any reason, then learn to create an alter ego in a parallel existence where you minimize your personal profile in the status quo world of mediocrity and stress so that your 'alter ego' can then flourish without all the limitations that you endure personally.

The alternative to taking on full personal responsibility and liability to all the compelled performance statutes is to cancel all contracts made in your personal name and start conducting your affairs through private trusts and business structures. Drop off the radar.

Another approach to this is to make a claim on the financial instruments created by your cestui-que-vie trust (JOHN DOE) and learn to be the creditor and not the debtor. This is a deep subject which I won't address here but there are solutions.

How do I pull out of the banking system?

Yes, you receive checks, you have to cash them, pay bills, use debit and credit cards etc.

There are ways to do all of that without using a local bank.

There are also ways of using a local bank account which is not in your name.

Now, whether you completely pull out of the banking system, or reduce your exposure, or simply restructure your current banking arrangements to get your name off the records is something you'll need to determine for yourself. Everyone's needs are different. We're not saying everyone just needs to close all accounts and walk away. That would not be advisable for most people.

But let me paint a general scenario for you;

What if you closed your personal accounts to remove all exposure to disclosures, seizures, garnishments and other forms of distraint and eliminate the concealed contracts hidden in your account opening agreements which exist with the US or NATION STATE who claims you as 'theirs'?

What if you replaced that personal account with a business account in the name of an LLC or Private Trust and it had its own EIN (Employer Identification Number)?

What if you only used that account to pay monthly bills and receive payments for your business/services and then other excess amounts not otherwise needed for monthly operations was sent to a safer and more private account without leaving a direct trail?

Let's say that the 'Private Account' was held in trust, managed by a professional, licensed trustee and when the trustee received the transfer of fiat currency, he could convert the fiat currency into a complete portfolio of 'alternative assets' according to your instructions.

What if the private account was in the name of a private trust, managed by the trustee and the asset portfolio, whatever it is, small or large, was domestic and international and not subject to any disclosure requirements or legal processes in your home country?

What if the trustee operated in such a way in which he/they were not subject to most forms of taxation and the trust corpus could grow entirely tax free?

What if all or part of the trust corpus could be held in precious metals in a private, non-bank, insured Swiss or Hong Kong vault and you had a debit card you could use to convert the gold holdings to spendable cash whenever you needed it for business expenses?

What if the trustees were in 4 different offshore jurisdictions the trust was in a 5th, the banking was in the 6th, 7th and 8th and assets were potentially held in the 9th and 10th or 11th depending on the size and nature of the portfolio? Would that be easy pickings for some lawsuit happy freeloader or bureau-rat with an over-inflated ego?

Wow! Put all of those 'What ifs' together and you'd have a pretty fantastic dream wouldn't you? Most would simply call it a far reaching fantasy and for all practical intents and purposes based on what's available from the status quo, they'd be right! Pure fantasy.

Pssst. Pssst! (in a whisper) come here! I have something for you…. It's not a dream and it's not a fantasy. It's a real situation and we know people doing this.

There are a number of private financial strategies involved and/or available with that situation but obviously, highly sensitive VIP strategies don't go into a book to be published and distributed worldwide. Those are reserved for our inner circle.

So yes, there are ways to walk away from the control, abuse and theft by the central bankers and their controlled minions, collectors and enforcers. It's 100% clean, legal and all above board. Nobody has ever gotten into trouble for doing clean business with transparent contracts and full supporting paperwork to provide checks and balances along the way.

Once the business/money travels 'over the horizon' it's never seen again by prying eyes who do not have a 'need to know'. Yet, as a functionary of the 'business' your access is as close as the nearest ATM.

Do you know which country is the world's largest tax haven? You might be surprised to know that it's the USA. Yes, it's the biggest tax haven in the world for 'foreigners'. It's own people are prisoners and slaves but foreigners are treated as kings! Yet another example of how the 5 Flag Concept can be so beneficial.

I have used so many attorneys over the years and it's sad to say that only 1 has been deemed worthy of my continued loyalty over the years. He also happens to have penned a book entitled 'HOW YOU CAN USE THE USA AS YOUR PERSONAL TAX HAVEN'. You'll find it on Amazon.

What's beautiful about the USA is that they force other countries to comply with ridiculous disclosure and reporting requirements back to the USA and in return, neither the USA nor the EU impose the same obligations on themselves to report to the rest of the world. It's a complete double standard. Do as I say, not as I do!

So why not at least have your 'money' become a foreigner, you put on your 'mystical magical teflon suit' and enjoy the benefits of the worlds largest tax haven right in your own back yard?

This world is screwed up, isn't it? Just gain some knowledge and you can make it work 'for you' rather than 'against you'.

> *Come out of her, my people, that ye be not partakers of her sins, and that ye receive not of her plagues.*
> *- Revelations. 18:4*

If any of these issues might be of interest, just follow the breadcrumbs found in the Appendix.

In the early 1980s, I wrote a book called 'The Complete Guide to Financial Privacy.' If I would write that book today, it would be a pamphlet. There is precious little privacy left.

- Mark Skousen

12

LIVING WITHOUT CREDIT REQUIRES BEING 'PROPERLY TRAINED'

Nearly the entire industrialized world has been sucked into the debt trap. Our discussion on the central banks has already addressed this. But as it relates to lifestyle, most people appear to have a lot of nice things; car, home, recreational vehicles, possibly a summer home, fancy furniture, nice neighborhood etc. You know the routine. And you know very well that the vast majority don't own a damn thing! Quite the contrary!

Because of being in servitude to the creditors, the debt masters *own them* and the debtors have to work double or triple hard just to 'maintain' the image of success when in fact they are debt slaves working for the bankers. Enough said.

So, here comes this guy from the states. He lost everything after being a political prisoner for a year or so. He comes out with little more than his custom tailored prison release clothes. He has no cash, no savings and no income and no job. He does what he has to for survival and starts with only some ideas and begins developing a business concept.

He had previously cancelled his SS-4 application/contract (Social Security Card) with the Social Security Administration and did the same with his Drivers License. So with no S.S. number/card, no drivers license and the only thing showing on his credit report was an old bankruptcy, he had no bank account, no credit and was living in other peoples' homes, let's just say he pretty much had 'no nothing' that ordinary people would say he would need to launch an effort at creating success!

What kind of a life would you project for someone like this?

What he did have was some friends and contacts. He had plenty of creativity. He had enthusiasm. He had knowledge and life experience and he had a burning desire to teach people the truth along with solutions to modern day problems.

He leveraged his contacts and experience to get him some good work doing training and asset protection for a forward thinking group working in 'alt-finance'. He was paid in cash.

He saved. He found a girl. Got married and within 18 months was on his way to Central America with a couple of shirts and a cute little dog.

So to make this really short, how does a guy like this find his way in a new country, where he doesn't speak the language well, he has no track record, no credit history, is new to town and the country and then he gets a mortgage for $300,000 to buy a 10 acre hacienda full of every imaginable fruit tree with huge pool, rancho and a house he completely remodeled and rebuilt into a tropical palace?

In this case, you've heard the phrase 'money talks' and that's the key. This guy was purchasing the property in the name of a company which he created and had good banking history and he put 30% of the property sale price

as a down payment PLUS he was able to show sufficient cash flow to the bank to assure them he could make the payment. It was that simple.
Of course, 'that guy' was me.

This place was so beautiful I thought I had died and gone to heaven. It was a true tropical paradise.

Fast forward a few years: Things aren't working out so well with the wife. She conspires with her lady friend who is the registered agent on the company, she sneaks into my office and takes the company bearer shares, and many other companies I was managing at the time. She has me removed from the bank accounts, cancels the Powers of Attorney I was operating on for the various companies and leaves me destitute and not even willing to talk. Nice!

No problem. At the time, I was overloaded with stress trying to manage too much and this relieved me of all of that. The first night out of the house on my own was the best night of sleep I've ever had.

What next?

Just like before: Start a new business, re-establish my banking, take my ideas, contacts, experience and enthusiasm and do it again, this time bigger and better and without the headache and interference of a 'wanna be' looking over my shoulder at every move. I make it sound easy but it wasn't. It took extreme perseverance, commitment, discipline and the attitude to continue forward during difficult times or die! This is what most people are missing these days, that 'Do or Die' attitude to keep on keeping on and never quit.

Now to the point of living without credit.

This second time around I didn't have the advantage of having savings and a chunk of cash I could just plunk down.

And if I did have it, I wouldn't be sinking it into dirt and bricks.

We've all heard about 'the time value of money'.

Consider yourself having to make a decision. The decision comes down to choosing one of two options. Say you have $100,000 in the bank (or any amount).

Option 1 is: You can sink it into real estate and buy a home giving it all to the bank/seller and then be broke again, or

Option 2 is: keep your nest egg, invest it in your business or in other high yielding opportunities and rent a beautiful palatial home to live in without having to make the huge investment and commitment.

It's not too hard to find opportunities in the international markets where you can generate 10% or more per month in passive investments. Or do the same or better in your own business.

Let's work the numbers. Instead of investing the $100,000 in a home which will be an anchor for you holding you down, your 10% monthly earnings on that same amount, if invested, would generate $10,000 a month and the seed capital remains.

That $10,000 a month pays the rent on a high end palatial Hacienda plus leaves you more than enough to live on and invest into your business to make it grow. If your return were only 2% on the $100k you still have enough for rent and some bills and you keep your $100k in the bank.

Here where I live now is without question one of the most beautiful places I've ever seen and I've been around. It's in the mountains, away from the riff-raff, surrounded by lush tropical vegetation and animals, spectacular views of the ocean and coastline 20 miles below, waterfalls, hiking trails and so much. It's a dream.

Being a renter I can pick up stakes and move when I want, I'm not tied down and in this locale, I've enjoyed living in several of the best homes in the area. I get bored. I like variety.

The real estate market here right now is soft so available homes are plentiful. I expect it to get even softer for the next few years. Currently I'm living in a $500,000 home with the most spectacular views in the world and what would you guess the rent to be? It's only $1000 a month. In the scenario above that would leave me an additional $9,000 a month to grow my business or re-invest.

One thing I've done is to use some of the extra cash and rent a penthouse apartment in the city where I can go and entertain and enjoy the benefits of a world class city, have business meetings in a comfortable setting and basically have the best of both worlds.

As a PT in such a place where the government isn't out to harass you or steal from you, I live better **without any credit** than most people do WITH tons of credit (and debt).

The key is doing your own 'Proper Transactions' and being a 'Previous Taxpayer' helps a little bit also.

Are you starting to see the light?

"Freedom is the open window through which pours the sunlight of the human spirit and human dignity." - Herbert Hoover

13

HARMONIZING LAW WITH 'PERFECT TRANSCENDENCE'

Most of us eventually come to realize at some point in life that finding harmony in all things is the key to peace and happiness. If you've studied the issue at all you know how important it is the we find the right 'frequencies' to use and tap into.

I've seen electrical frequency generators heal physical ailments. I've seen colored light beams do the same to physical problems deep inside the body. What is light? Frequency! What is the difference between blue light and red light? Frequency!

Dogs and other animals can sense and hear frequencies which humans just physically cannot. We all have seen TV shows with stories of ghosts or spirits being able to pass through walls with ease and many marvel at this. But they are operating on a different frequency which is not hindered by the low frequency of the mass of a physical object.

Those who are more spiritually in tune with God and the universe will often talk about a certain sensitivity they have which gives them the ability to tap into a higher frequency. We all have this capability innately within us and it's simply matter of awareness and development.

With these concepts in mind then, we can talk about the bulky, clumsy control systems of man and his governments being similar to the low frequency of physical mass, say a block of wood or stone.

For those who want to rise above it, it then becomes a matter that we fine tune our awareness, knowledge, discipline and physical and legal positioning to find the correct frequencies whereby, like the spirits effortlessly traversing through walls of a house, you can effortlessly traverse the walls of control.

So let's bring it back down to earth and practical matters. By now it should be crystal clear that the single most salient characteristic of a successful PT is that he escapes most if not all local regulations and obligations wherever he is simply due to the fact that he appears as though he is from 'somewhere else'. He doesn't belong in the group known as 'local citizens' or 'residents'.

And as you will see shortly, if you walk as a follower of Jesus, you really don't belong to this 'World'. You operate on a different level living in the spiritual realm and not so much the physical.

The rationale for that is simple. Regardless of where you live or under which flag, the traits of Central Government (that block of wood you need to traverse) are always the same;

- Demands supreme jurisdiction
- Develops into a self willed entity, the people notwithstanding.
- Has its own personality (unchallenged authority and force)
- Must protect itself with force and coercion to survive
- Is never a servant, but rather a master
- Is perpetually at war with the public
- Uses police and corrupt courts to enforce its will

- Uses debt, threat, brutality and brainwashing against the people among other weapons to ensure compliance.
- Uses a central bank, a central tax collector, a central welfare system, a centrally controlled police system and a government licensed education system to keep the people subjugated.

Now, under those conditions, who wouldn't want to be 'from somewhere else'? You don't have to think too hard about that one.

To see how we live today and where we are headed, we only have to look back into history to see that we are repeating the exact same scenario that occurred in the Bible with the history of the tower of Babel.

In the days of Babylon men thought that they could build a tower tall enough to reach the heavens thus putting man on a par with God.

Today, sorry souls are using technology to create hideous distortions and interventions in nature (CERN, DNA splicing, genetic re-engineering, etc.), preparing to merge man and machine so that men can be 'super human' with capabilities better than what God created and so man can live virtually forever with implanted technology and surpass the divine plan God had for us. In this line of thinking, man becomes his own God and then doesn't need God. Pure folly. Why would any rational creature want any part of that?

In today's world we are re-living history to the 'T'.

I told you about my experience as an Ambassador to the Embassy of Heaven and how I destroyed and returned my state issued papers and obtained my new 'papers' from the Embassy of Heaven church. This prompted me to dig deeper into this issue to expand my knowledge seeking those higher frequencies.

In ONE FREEMANS WAR... I filled 13 pages of the appendix with selected biblical scriptures all relating to Revelations 18:4 "Come out of her my people and do not share in her sins so as to not share in her plagues."

I won't repeat those 13 pages here. Hopefully you can get that book and learn a lot from it as well.

But two of my (many) favorites are;

- 1 Corinthians 7:21: "were you a slave when called? If you can gain your freedom do it. For he who is called in the Lord as a slave is a freedman of the Lord."

- II Corinthians 10:3: "For though we live in the world we are not carrying on a worldly war for the weapons of our warfare are not worldly but have divine power to destroy strongholds (other frequencies). We destroy arguments and every proud obstacle to the knowledge of God and take every thought captive to obey Christ, being ready to punish every disobedience when your obedience is complete."

Now let's ponder those scriptures. What do they say to you? Don't they say;

1. You have a choice, be a slave to man or be a freedman unto the Lord? Check
2. As a freedman (PT) we are 'in' the world, be we are not 'of' (belong to) the world? Check
3. With our PT positioning and with the power of the Holy Spirit in us, our weapons of knowledge, spirit and purpose have the power to destroy arguments and strongholds. What you've read up until this point in my various exploits breaking through one wall after another is a clear indication that I have destroyed those

strongholds which have been built to fence us in and control us and I have done it with regularity. Check

4. No argument can stand on its own against us. We rise above the tricks and traps of control and subjugation. All it requires is knowledge and obedience to Jesus. With that, HIS blessings and hand of protection are upon us. Remember my pleas to 'make me invisible' when I was in my car with 'Heaven' plates at the stoplights in Oklahoma City with cop cars and sheriffs deputies swirling all around me? I was invisible and was never hassled. I tapped into a frequency and rose above my earthly situation.

So the key to being a successful PT is clear. All of the tips, strategies, positioning discussed in previous chapters are the 'mechanics' which form the machine.

Your spiritual strength comes from knowing who you are as a son or daughter in Jesus, being obedient and receiving HIS blessings. **This is the fuel which powers the mechanical engine you've built.** They must work together for ultimate success as defined in this book.

Now, I know that some people who are not well informed will always come forward and challenge me saying that I will put people in jail with this information. Hogwash. People are already going to jail for no good reason and I have nothing to do with that. And that will continue regardless.

This happens every day because they do not know who they are and are ignorant of how they should be handling themselves. That's the reality we face. You are already in jeopardy by doing nothing. Your only hope is to take bold action to be free!

Take a low profile (not like me) and escape scrutiny which is the entire purpose of this book. So don't get confused.

This position is not to put one in conflict with the present day authorities. In fact, when you do things correctly there can be mutual respect and harmony, at least for a time. But don't forget that we are in the end times and true Christians will be martyred en masse anyway. That's prophecy unfolding, not some little book on the PT lifestyle! Sorry, but this book is not going to change biblical prophesy!

In view of that, let me share with you a little research I put together which I think you might appreciate. It is intended to be the basis to put public servants, court officials etc. on notice of 'foreign status' and it uses a mix of biblical scripture to reference my law and the statutory code to reference the law which binds *them* in their official capacity. Amazingly my law also binds them in their personal capacity. Read this and be thinking about harmony and frequencies.

Affidavit - Declaration of Status

Know ye, to all whom shall come upon me or consider the essence of whom you are dealing with, that I :

Marcus Edwin Orelius

...being duly appointed to my mission (22 USC § 254) as an Ambassador from the Embassy of Heaven under the guidance and direction of our Lord Jesus the Christ, and being recognized and protected as an Ambassador for a Sovereign Kingdom foreign to the UNITED STATES, the STATE OF COLORADO, and/or any of their/its subdivisions, pursuant to UNITED STATES Public Law 97-280 found at 96 Statutes at Large 1211 (sessions laws), which gives official recognition and deference by the UNITED STATES to my Sovereign, HIS laws and jurisdiction and subsequently by the United States Congress passing Public Law 79-291 the International Organizations Immunities Act which further recognizes the inherent status and immunity which travels with me, I do hereby affirm under the penalties of bearing false witness, the following facts to be true, complete, correct and not misleading and that I am of legal age and sound mind, to wit;

As Ambassador appointed by my Sovereign as per, among others, Rev. 1:6, Ex 19:6, Isa 61:6, II Cor.: 5:20;

1. I am appointed to my station as a sojourner upon the land/kingdom created by my sovereign (the entirety of earth), traveling through this territory/state/nation on a temporary basis and I do not have a permanent residence.
2. I do not 'reside' in nor do I 'do business' or 'vote' in THE STATE OF COLORADO
3. I am not employed, I am not un-employed and I am not employable under the general usages of those terms as I am not engaged in commerce.
4. I derive no benefit or franchise from the UNITED STATES or the STATE OF COLORADO and thus have no contractual entanglements.
5. I have no income or property situated in, or derived from the STATE OF COLORADO or the UNITED STATES.
6. I am not engaged in commercial transport for hire in the STATE OF COLORADO and thus have no driver license, nor is one required from those with diplomatic status.
7. I have no Social Security number and again am not engaged in commerce.
8. That in addition to my exempt status as Ambassador, being a sojourner upon the land, passing through and not being 'resident in', nor 'doing business in' the STATE OF COLORADO, the automobile I use is not eligible to be 'registered' as other commercial vehicles are for state

residents. The law does not provide for registration of non-commercial vehicles by non-residents who are not licensed nor engaged in business in the STATE OF COLORADO and it cannot be held to those standards by law. The law does not require the impossible. The identification plates used are self explanatory and exempt. The vehicle is registered in the Embassy of Heaven registry for public safety with the number: 123456789

9. I offer no surety, nor am I guarantor for any other entity or person whether they be real or fictitious.
10. I am prepared to provide a complete memorandum of law upon request on the above, for clarity of the issues, rights and responsibilities of any or all parties involved, or wishing to be involved with me.

The above is true. Correct and complete to the best of my knowledge and further this affiant sayeth naught, on this the ____ day of ____ in the year of our Lord, 2018 A.D.

_____

Marcus Edwin Orelius – Ambassador at Large
Embassy of Heaven, Kingdom of Jesus the Christ
Seal

Notice & Demand

This information is intended for all public servants for 'THE STATE' in whatever Department or subdivision you might represent. This is a good faith notice of status in accordance with the law which you are subject to. Your law prescribes some very specific limitations on the authority you might try to exert and I present you with this Fair Notice in good faith to help you avoid creating any personal liability for damages which might ensue from your misapplication of the law, as it relates to me.

I hereby respectfully remind you to honor your responsibility to the law and your contract (oath of office) and leave me unhindered to proceed in peace according to my mission and mandate.

With that, I wish you peace and many blessings.

So then we have the 'Memorandum of Law in Support' bringing up the Foreign Sovereign Immunities Act.

Memorandum of Law in Support of
'Affidavit & Declaration of Status'
as Ambassador under Foreign Law

This memorandum is the fundamental baseline upon which I, Marcus Edwin Orelius, adhere to and conduct myself in my personal affairs and official duties as Ambassador for the Embassy of Heaven, on behalf of my Sovereign which is 'foreign law' to the UNITED STATES, the STATES and their political subdivisions.

This memorandum and its contents, being public knowledge available to everyone everywhere, merely serves as a reminder and that these matters and this document are self authenticating and are 'res judicata'.

Governing Law & Sovereignty:
There can only be one absolute sovereign and king. Samuel Adams, one of the founding fathers of the united States of America said, "Sovereignty is a theological word, not a political one." He objected to the use of the word in the political arena and he did so rightly because only God is sovereign. There is nothing else nor anyone else who can claim that status legitimately. Thus, 'the state' cannot claim this authority of sovereignty and it must serve

the one true sovereign which is the kingdom which I serve and to which I owe allegiance.

Timothy 6:15, '….He is the blessed and only potentate, the king of kings.'

Psalm 75:6-7 'For promotion cometh neither from the east, nor from the west, nor from the south. But God is the judge, he putteth down one and setteth up another.'

Proverbs 8:15-16, 'By me, kings reign and princes decree justice, by me princes rule, and nobles, even all judges of the earth.'

God created all creatures and <u>all men have equal standing</u> before God. None can rule over others by 'divine right', by 'compelled performance statutes' nor by 'threat' of force or imprisonment.

Galatians 5:1, 'Stand fast therefore in the liberty wherewith Christ has made us free, and be not entangled again with the yoke of bondage,' (i.e. indentured servitude, debt slaves, chattel and/or guarantors, debtors & sureties for any 'persons')

I, along with my brothers and sisters, are children of the Most High. Our service is to a much higher authority than that of earthly kingdoms. And since we cannot serve two masters, (Matthew 6:24, Luke 16:13) my Affidavit and Declaration of Status reflects whom I serve and the laws I must obey which are of a jurisdiction which is unique and exclusive to any other. Therefore, based upon the facts and my willful election of the applicable law, I am not a 'person' to be subject to, or regulated by, the state.

Men (the state) cannot give rights. All government can do is to recognize and secure those rights ordained by God. Therefore, I issue this…

Notice of Contract

All public servants for corporate government who have sworn an oath of office in the united States of America and/or it's many states, counties and subdivisions, have sworn to protect and preserve the constitution of the united States of America, which does not grant any rights. It restricts government agents from violating my natural, God given rights which pre-existed the birth of government and are superior to and inalienable from encroachments and cannot be regulated. To all public servants of foreign governments: I accept your oath of office and the underlying constitution to which you have sworn your allegiance to, as a binding contract with me, a natural, freeborn child of God. This shall be your governing law, superior to and superseding all others.

Official Recognition in United States Law:

The foreign government of the United States recognized the sovereignty of God by enacting :

Public Law 97-280 (96 Stat. 1211).

By means of this joint resolution, Congress declared the Bible to be the Divine Word of God and authorized the President to proclaim 1983 as the "Year of the Bible", which was approved on October 04, 1982. Since now, public law recognizes the Word of God, it must acknowledge all things therein to include his statutes, commandments, and judgments and as such, as a separate body politic.

A public law is not just a simple declaration of Congress or a declaration of public policy. A public law applies to the people generally of a nation, in contradistinction to a private law (corporate statutes applying only to members, officials and persons contracted to the municipal corporation known as 'state' or 'federal' government).

A public law is the law of the land. Thus, in declaring Public Law 97-280, Congress has opened the door by recognizing '…the value of voluntarily applying the teachings of Holy Scriptures…" in the Kingdom of God.

Knowing well that one cannot serve two masters, Congress opened the door to God's people who wanted to follow this path and serve their Sovereign in accordance with HIS law.

Congress, comprehending very well that the people with this status are in fact and in law, separate and apart from all other 'legal persons' who are beholden to the municipal corporation and its statutory compelled performance statutes and regulations.

God's people live upon the land and within the national borders of the geographic 50 states of the union of the united states of America, but in fact are without the UNITED STATES or the United States and thus, in implementing this Public Law, it recognizes this important fact.

> Public Law 97-280
> 97th Congress
>
> ### Joint Resolution
>
> Authorizing and requesting the President to proclaim 1983 as the "Year of the Bible".
>
> Oct. 4, 1982
> [S.J. Res. 165]
>
> Whereas the Bible, the Word of God, has made a unique contribution in shaping the United States as a distinctive and blessed nation and people;
>
> Whereas deeply held religious convictions springing from the Holy Scriptures led to the early settlement of our Nation;
>
> Whereas Biblical teachings inspired concepts of civil government that are contained in our Declaration of Independence and the Constitution of the United States;
>
> Whereas many of our great national leaders—among them Presidents Washington, Jackson, Lincoln, and Wilson—paid tribute to the surpassing influence of the Bible in our country's development, as in the words of President Jackson that the Bible is "the rock on which our Republic rests";
>
> Whereas the history of our Nation clearly illustrates the value of voluntarily applying the teachings of the Scriptures in the lives of individuals, families, and societies;
>
> Whereas this Nation now faces great challenges that will test this Nation as it has never been tested before; and
>
> Whereas that renewing our knowledge of and faith in God through Holy Scripture can strengthen us as a nation and a people: Now, therefore, be it
>
> *Resolved by the Senate and House of Representatives of the United States of America in Congress assembled,* That the President is authorized and requested to designate 1983 as a national "Year of the Bible" in recognition of both the formative influence the Bible has been for our Nation, and our national need to study and apply the teachings of the Holy Scriptures.
>
> Year of the Bible.
>
> Approved October 4, 1982.

This clearly indicates that Congress has acknowledged that there are men and women like me who are subjects of the Kingdom of Heaven and God's written word. This is significant, in that Congress has recognized this distinct class of people and has made this statutory provision to protect those people in this kingdom, who live and operate under the law of the realm which is separate and apart from, and foreign to, the United States.

What is a separate and distinct nation? A body of individuals who operate according to a commonly recognized set of laws and from which, violations of those laws have their own separate and peculiar penalties or judgments.

NATIONS. *Nations or states are independent bodies politic; societies of men united together for the purpose of promoting their mutual safety and advantage by the joint efforts of their combined strength.*

2. But every combination of men who govern themselves, independently of all others, will not be considered a nation; a body of pirates, for example, who govern themselves, are not a nation. To constitute a nation another ingredient is required. <u>*The body thus formed must respect other nations in general, and each of their members in particular*</u>*. Such a society has her affairs and her interests; she deliberates and takes resolutions in common; thus becoming a moral person who possesses an understanding and will peculiar to herself, and is susceptible of obligations and rights. Vattel, Prelim. §1, 2; 5 Pet. S. C. R. 52. (From Bouviers – 1856)*

The Unites States Congress, by recognizing *"...the national need to study and apply the scriptures."* did not issue a mandate, but rather opened the door for 'de jure' Americans to seek refuge from the corporate body politic with its regulations and compelled performance statutes in order to preserve the essence of their nature along with the inherent rights and liberties associated with that nature. This is clear because *'...studying and applying the scriptures'* can only mean one thing: <u>submitting to that authority and none other</u>. Again, when applied, the scriptures are clear: one cannot serve two masters.

By stating that *"...The Word of God has made a unique contribution in shaping the United States..."* this Public Law 97-280 further establishes that, from its inception, the UNITED STATES has been fundamentally involved with, and inextricably linked to, God's Kingdom/Kingdom of Heaven as a foreign organization (Holy Scripture being a set of laws honored, respected and enforced in a regimen separate and apart from the legislative statutes of the United States.)

Earthly Matters – Sovereign Immunity in the Political Realm

Having acknowledged its involvement in, and reliance upon, this foreign organization, the United States congress has further enacted :

The International Organizations Immunities Act, Public Law 79-291: codified at **22 USC § 288**

Wherein, "For the purposes of this title, the term "international organization" means a public international organization in which the United States participates pursuant to any treaty or under the authority of any Act of Congress..." (as in PL 97-280)

..."SEC. 2.

    International organizations shall enjoy the status, immunities, exemptions, and privileges set forth in this section, as follows:

a) International organizations shall, to the extent consistent with the instrument creating them, possess the capacity—

    (i) to contract;

    (ii) to acquire and dispose of real and personal property;

    (iii) to institute legal proceedings.

b) International organizations, their property and their assets, wherever located, and by whomsoever held, shall enjoy the same immunity from suit and every form of judicial process as is enjoyed by foreign governments, except to the extent that such organizations may expressly waive their immunity for the purpose of any proceedings or by the terms of any contract.

c) Property and assets of international organizations, wherever located and by whomsoever held, shall be immune from search, unless such immunity be expressly waived, and from confiscation. The archives of international organizations shall be inviolable.

d) Insofar as concerns customs duties and internal-revenue taxes imposed upon or by reason of importation, and the procedures in connection therewith; the registration of foreign agents; and the treatment of official communications, the privileges, exemptions, and immunities to which international organizations shall be entitled shall be those accorded under similar circumstances to foreign governments.

And further, we can look at the:

FOREIGN SOVEREIGN IMMUNITIES ACT at 28 USC §§ 1602-1611

Since I am a natural man, living and breathing upon the land at the behest of my creator and sovereign, I vehemently deny and disavow ever willingly and knowingly being a 'legal person' as is clearly confirmed in my affidavit (separate from this document).

However, in the event that one would like to argue to the contrary, they then would have to deal with the fact that I am a natural born American, with family heritage roots in America going back to the original 13 colonies which predate the corporate UNITED STATES and its subsequent bankruptcy which has been administered to, for and on behalf of all 'United States Citizens' since HJR 192 in 1933.

Thus, the FOREIGN SOVEREIGN IMMUNITIES ACT at 28 USC §§ 1602-1611 would restrict all public servants of the corporate body politic who are involved in administering the bankruptcy, as it relates to their dealings with me, and all those men and women descendants of the original colonies and the subsequent organic de jure republic who are not members of, and are foreign to, the UNITED STATES, the United States and/or the United States of America with all subdivisions, agents and agencies.

Specifically, I point to §1604– **Immunity of a Foreign State from Jurisdiction** wherein it is clearly stated that *"...a foreign state shall be immune from the jurisdiction of the courts of the United States and of the States..."*

And whereas, the current administrators of the bankruptcy of the United States, et al, do not and cannot recognize law, substance or any of the Acts or decisions of the 'de jure' united States of America prior to HJR 192, to the contrary, the foreign law of my realm predates and supercedes all forms of government and said 'universal' law always was and always will be immutable and unchanged, thereby clearly demonstrating it's unique and superior nature and character which is foreign to all earthly governments.

And insofar as this goes, learned men working in my realm along with the body politic of their contemporaries at the time, which predated the United States, reflect this reality in the following examples;

Robin v. Hardaway, 1 Jefferson 109, 114, 1 Va. Reports Ann. 58, 61 (1772) aff'd. *Gregory v. Baugh,* **29 Va. 681, 29 Va. Rep. Ann. 466, 2 Leigh 665 (1831)** *"Now all acts of legislature apparently contrary to natural right and justice, are, in our laws, and must be in the nature of things, considered as void. The laws of nature are the laws of God;* <u>**whose authority can be superseded by no power on earth**</u>. *A legislature must not obstruct our obedience to him from whose punishments they cannot protect us. All human constitutions which contradict his laws, we are in conscience* *bound to disobey. Such have been the adjudications of our courts of justice.* **"And cited 8 Co. 118. a. Bonham's case. Hob. 87; 7. Co. 14. a. Calvin's case**

Dr. Bonham's Case, *8 Coke's Reports 107, at 118* (1610) *"[I]n many cases, the common law will control acts of parliament, and sometimes adjudge them to be utterly void: for when an act of parliament is against common right and reason, or repugnant, or impossible to be performed, the common law will control it, and adjudge such to be void."*; **aff'd. *Robin v. Hardaway,* 1 Jefferson 109, 114, 1 Va. Reports Ann. 58, 61 (1772);**

McFaul v. Ramsey 61 U.S. (20 How.) 523, 525, 15 L.Ed. 1010, 1011 (1858) *"This system, matured by the wisdom of ages, founded on principles of truth and sound reason, has been ruthlessly abolished in many of our states, who have rashly substituted in its place the suggestions of scholiasts who invent new codes and systems of pleadings to order. But this attempt to abolish all species, and establish a single genus, is found to be beyond the power of legislative omnipotence. They cannot compel the human mind not to distinguish between things that differ."*

So whereas, the UNITED STATES and its bankruptcy administrators with their agents generally seek to treat all people born upon the land and residing within its geographic borders equally as subject 'citizens', this qualifies as a willful act of genocide in an attempt to eliminate an entire class of people which is in direct contradistinction to McFaul v. Ramsey above.

Citizenship & Appointment:

My appointment as Ambassador for the Embassy of Heaven is evidenced by:

1) the unrebuted affidavit which I have affirmed under penalties of bearing false witness (the law of my realm) filed into the public record at Book __ Volume__ Page ___ of the ____ County Recorders office only as a means of delivering public notice for the benefit of the public and not myself.
2) My passport, issued by the governing authority which is the Embassy of Heaven and which is an official declaration of my status.

And further, by declaring the '…need to study and apply the law of the Holy Scriptures…', the United States Congress along with the Embassy of Heaven both concur that this scripture referenced below, having been 'voluntarily applied' as per PL 97-280 makes my status very clear in no uncertain terms, to wit;

Ambassador appointment: 2 Corinthians 5:20, "We are ambassadors for Christ, as though God were pleading through us: we implore you on Christ's behalf, be reconciled to God."

Citizenship confirmed: by; Philippians 3:20, "…but our citizenship is in heaven…" and Ephesians 2:19, "So then you are no longer foreigners and strangers, but fellow citizens with the saints, and members of God's household"

Royal Priesthood: 1 Peter 2:9, "We are a chosen generation, a royal priesthood, a holy nation, His own special people."

Ministerial Function: "But ye shall be named the priests of the LORD: men shall call you the ministers of our LORD:… Isa 61:6

Bestowal of Kingdom: Luke 22:29 Jesus said to His apostles, "I bestow upon you a kingdom, just as My Father bestowed one upon Me, who delivered us out of the power of darkness, and translated us into the kingdom of the Son of his love; - Col. 1:13

Supreme Law of the Land. "You shall love the LORD your God with all your heart, with all your soul, and with all your mind. This is the first and great commandment. And the second is like it: You shall love your neighbor as yourself. On these two commandments hang all the Law and the Prophets." (Matthew 22:37-40)

Kingdom of Heaven Exists Now. The time is fulfilled, and the kingdom of God is at hand. Repent, and believe in the gospel. (Mark 1:15)

Authority for Using Highways. Jesus commanded His followers saying, "All authority has been given to Me in heaven and on earth. Go therefore and make disciples of all the nations, baptizing them in the name of the Father and of the Son and of the Holy Spirit, teaching them to observe all things that I have commanded you; and lo, I am with you always, even to the end of the age." (Matthew 28:18-20)

Ownership of Highways. The earth is the LORD'S and all its fullness. "I am God, your God! Every beast of the forest is mine, and the cattle on a thousand hills. I know all the birds of the mountains, and the wild beasts of the field are Mine. If I were hungry, I would not tell you; for the world is Mine, and all its fullness." (1 Corinthians 10:26; Psalm 50:7,10-12)

Receiving Christ's little ones. Jesus Christ said, "Whoever receives one of these little children in My name receives Me; and whoever receives Me, receives not Me but Him who sent Me. Whoever gives you a cup of water to drink in My name, because you belong to Christ, assuredly, I say to you, he will by no means lose his reward." (Mark 9:37,41)

Warning for those who cause stumbling.
Jesus Christ said, "Whoever causes one of these little ones who believe in Me to stumble, it would be better for him if a millstone

were hung around his neck, and he were thrown into the sea." (Mark 9:42)

Rejection of the Gospel of the Kingdom.
Jesus Christ said, "Whatever city you enter, and they do not receive you, go out into its streets and say, 'The very dust of your city which clings to us we wipe off against you. Nevertheless know this, that the kingdom of God has come near you.' But I say to you that it will be more tolerable in that Day for Sodom than for that city. He who hears you hears Me, he who rejects you rejects Me, and he who rejects Me rejects Him who sent Me." (Luke 10:10-12,16)

Free Exercise of Faith
The 'Free Exercise' clause of the First Amendment to the constitution for the united States of America (public servants contract with the people) reads:

"Congress shall make no law respecting an establishment of religion, or prohibiting the free exercise thereof..."

This is absolute with no qualifiers or exceptions. Thus was born the doctrine of 'Separation of church and state'. State actors have no authority to interfere with my ministerial activities which are 'everything I do'.

In Personam Jurisdiction
Putting aside the issues of foreign law and diplomatic immunities for a moment, we can look directly at the subject of 'In Personam' Jurisdiction.

The state has an obvious jurisdiction over those persons 'of the state' subject to its jurisdiction.

There are two types of persons;
1) the natural person who is a walking talking man and woman upon the land who is created by God, and

2) artificial persons which are 'personas fictas' which are created by the state which is a juridical or artificial person (Latin: **persona ficta**; also 'juristic person') has a legal name and has certain rights, protections, privileges, responsibilities, and liabilities in law, similar to those of a natural person. The concept of a juridical person is a fundamental legal fiction.

The creator always has original jurisdiction of that which he creates.

I am created by God as a natural man, thus the Kingdom of Heaven has 'in personam jurisdiction' over me.

I am not a 'persona ficta' and am not created by the state. Thus, the state has no 'in personam' jurisdiction over me.

I obey the laws of God and HE is my Lord and Master.

"Know ye not, that to whom ye yield yourselves servants to obey, his servants ye are whom ye obey; whether of sin unto death, or of obedience unto righteousness?" Romans 6:16

Subject Matter Jurisdiction
The state has codified its laws subject to its constitution and these are the rules for those 'persons' who are subject to its jurisdiction. Likewise, the Bible is the constitution for the Kingdom of Heaven which is recognized by Congress supra.

Since the law is the thing which connects its sovereign with its people and each body of law contains its own unique penalties and remedies for sins against that law, it's quite clear that the subject matter jurisdiction of the Kingdom of Heaven is quite separate and distinct from that of 'The State'.

One does not have subject matter jurisdiction over the other and its subjects must be dealt with accordingly in their respective venues.

"Now therefore, if ye will obey my voice indeed, and keep my covenant (law), then ye shall be a peculiar treasure unto me above all people: for all the earth is mine." Ex 19:5, (See also Deut 32:8, 1 Kings 8:53)

"And ye shall be unto me a kingdom of priests, and a holy nation." Ex 19:6 (See also 1 Pet 2:5-9, Deut 7:6)

Being obedient to his voice is being obedient to his commandments, laws, statutes and judgments which is HIS covenant. There will be no 'kingdom of priests' in God's "holy nation" for those who obey the laws of 'another' nation.

God has mandated his chosen people to follow and obey the laws of HIS Kingdom. These laws, HIS Word, is perfect and need not be added to and keeping them brings rewards. The Word (law) of God states;

"The law of the LORD is perfect, converting the soul: the testimony of the LORD is sure, making wise the simple."
"The statutes of the LORD are right, rejoicing the heart: the commandment of the LORD is pure, enlightening the eyes."

"The fear of the LORD is clean, enduring forever: the judgments of the LORD are true and righteous altogether."
"More to be desired are they than gold, yea, than much find gold: sweeter also than honey and the honeycomb."
Moreover by them is thy servant warned: in keeping of them is great reward." – Psalms 19:7-11

> *"I will put my law in their inward parts, and in their heart will I write it; and I will be their God, and they shall be my people." - Jer 31:33, Heb 8:8-10*

As a citizen of and Ambassador for the Kingdom of Heaven, I can only obey those laws of HIS Kingdom. This was well understood by the forefathers of the united states of America who expressed similar sentiments. George Mason expressed the prevailing sentiment of the colonists when he cited Coke and argued that both the people and the judges are:

> *"...in conscience bound to disobey all enactments which contradict the laws of nature and the laws of God. The laws of nature are the laws of God, whose authority can be superseded by no power on earth. A legislature must not obstruct our obedience to HIM, from whose punishment they cannot protect us. All humans which contradict HIS laws, we are conscience bound to disobey."*

In conclusion: This memorandum is not a complete treatise on the subject, but should suffice to properly establish the lawful basis of my Affidavit and Declaration of Status and shall serve as proper and due Notice to any and all who may have an alleged claim or interest in me or my activities.

Go in Peace.

———————End of document———————

Now, this document serves no purpose if your life arrangements do not support its contentions.

In other words if you continue to live with;

- State issued drivers license
- Social security number on everything
- Registered street address for mail delivery
- Employee contributions to all government social systems
- Business licenses
- Professional licenses
- Registrations in your name
- And all the trappings of a 'resident' 'citizen',

These would contradict everything declared in the affidavit and you have proven yourself a fraud. Don't just start waving documents thinking they are magic. You have to support them, you have to defend them and you have to 'live' them to have any impact.

So in conclusion, you will be a slave to man, or a freedman in Jesus and isn't it wonderful that you have a choice?

If you've studied this chapter well you can see that an honest PT can honor both God's law and mans law and have them both be in harmony side by side. When you know it well enough there can be no arguments which will stand against you as you are protected by both sets of law. Now that sure sounds like 'Transcending to a Perfect Frequency' doesn't it?

14

LIVING FREE IN 'PEACEFUL TRANQUILITY'

Imagine for a moment putting yourself in the following scenario;

You get up in the morning at any hour which suits you. You roll into your shorts, t-shirt and slippers and go make a strong cup of Colombian coffee. From there you take your coffee out to the terrace to sit and play with your dogs who never miss a chance to show you how much they love you. While sipping your coffee you look out over the Pacific coastline 25 miles below you while the rising sun shimmers off the water like a self illuminating display.

Low lying clouds representing the remainder of the moist night air, intermittently fill the valleys below and hug the hills like a blanket of cotton laying on the carpet of green foliage. The morning sun brings out the colors of the numerous varieties of tropical flowers around you and the birds are happily chirping and squawking as they flit about with energy and joy.

Nearby you hear the distinct sound of your neighborhood Toucans as if they are trying to get your attention.

The beauty and peace in your soul reminds you of what God has provided for all of us to enjoy in his beautiful creation. You feel a unity in spirit with the universe and take the opportunity to expand that with prayer and meditation giving thanks for your blessings and praying for those who have not yet found that peace so that they soon will.

Still in pajamas and slippers you mosey on over to the home office and begin working on projects and reaching out to the world.

Due to your legal and financial positioning as a 'PT' you have the time and financial freedom to be creative writing books, creating videos, expressing yourself in ways which are as meaningful as you can make them.

You are so engrossed in your work that before you know it, you look up at the clock and it's already 2:30 in the afternoon. You break for some breakfast long after lunchtime.

Now it's time to play with the dogs again and take a siesta in the hammock with a cool breeze in your face and your special princess in your lap in the hammock.

You go back and work for a bit more before it's time for happy hour. A refreshing and well made drink with a snack brings some relaxation and an opportunity to shrug off the emotional burdens that the world puts on you as you have to deal with it. The hammock again serves its purpose very well and the sun has now shifted from its morning position to give an entirely different look to your view of the coastline and mountains around you.

As the daylight wanes you put on the evening lights around the house giving it a warm ambiance. And as the evening approaches you decide how to spend the evening hours; reading, working, making a nice dinner, or cranking up the jacuzzi for a well deserved aqua massage and glass of wine to unwind after a 'hard day'.

By being debt free and a 'Previous Taxpayer' you have extra money to help the local kids in various projects. You can support their sports teams to keep them off the streets or assist in providing for education or special training which they can't get anywhere else. In other words you can take kids who really would have little chance in life due to the lack of education, resources and mentorship and give them some hope to help balance the scales a bit so they might actually have a chance to do better. And of course there is no end in opportunities to help others in many ways.

Perhaps you could use a change-up from the life in your tropical paradise and a couple days per week in the city is just what the doctor ordered. Your involvement in different groups brings endless opportunities to make new friends and talk with other ex-pats who have a much better understanding of how the world works than some of the hillbillies back home. Sharing experiences and insights with them always makes for a fun night out These are people you can talk to and they actually have a clue about what's happening in the real world.

Your visit gives you a chance to enjoy a luxury hotel, room service, world class chefs and the better things that life has to offer.

When you've had your fill, you return to your garden paradise of peace and tranquility.

Could you imagine living like that? Is it just a dream?

Yes, it is a dream. It's my dream and I'm living it.

This is my life as a 'PT'.

15

CONCLUSION: THIS BOOK IS 'PREMATURELY TERMINATED'

There is so much material to cover but this will have to suffice for now.

There is no question that life is an adventure with some extreme challenges. Nobody escapes those tests and we all have our own battles to fight. Pure gold only comes into existence when the dross has been burned off with extreme heat. For us to have the will, the strength and the courage of tempered steel, we must first pass through the fire. Success comes at a price which is not always measured in dollars.

Do not fear obstacles. With Jesus as your silent partner, any obstacle can be overcome. You don't have to rely on your own limited knowledge or capabilities. Move forward with boldness, conviction and faith and HE'll do the rest. I've proven that.

Here's one thing my experience has taught me which is not what most people would expect. I learned not to fear things like a little jail time. If you are properly set up and with the right mind-set it can be a blessing giving you time to do things you wouldn't otherwise have time to do! Plus, you meet some very interesting people there! We all have fear of the unknown. Once you go to jail for the first time, you'll know it better and it won't be so scary and the threat of sending you to jail will not intimidate you. You won't bow down to the threat and sell yourself out.

Do not fear losing money or property. I've lost everything, and I mean 'everything' 3 times in my life. My attitude is: "Money comes and money goes but God always provides. It was never mine to begin with. He who gives, can take it back. What's important is to protect your soul. Keep it pure. Protect it from being polluted. 'Things' are irrelevant. Keep moving forward."

This book represents nearly 40 years of experience with plenty of trial and error, tests and challenges.

With that in mind there is no guarantee that the ideas expressed in the contents of this book will work for you or that they would do anything for you. The noose put around our necks by the controllers is tightening day by day and the world is changing rapidly.

However some things remain constant and never change, such as;

- it doesn't matter how many changes there are in statutory code or how complicated or draconian they get. It doesn't matter so long as you know 'who' they apply to and that you're positioned to be sure that you're not one of those 'Persons'.
- All law emanates from the top. Be obedient to that simple code of conduct and you'll have all the enforcers you need to protect and assist you from this world and beyond.
- No system of government in the history of the world has ever been successful squelching man's desire to be free. In the end freedom always prevails, but not without a price.
- The 'maxims of law' remain constant. Look them up and know them well.

Lastly, it's important to understand that what I've discussed in this book is not an 'All or Nothing' proposition. You don't just cut the cords and go cold turkey overnight. What I did was a step by step process which started many years go and continues to this very day.

Like every journey, it starts with the first step!

Remember, while we are 'in' this world, we are not 'of' this world. Seek your new kingdom where a place has been prepared for you in freedom and love with all things provided.

> *"The truth is not for all men, but only for those who seek it."*
> *- Ayn Rand*

"For the kingdom of God does not consist of talk, but of POWER."

- 1 Corinthians 4:20

Amen!

APPENDIX

Other Books By Mark on Amazon

ONE FREEMANS WAR...
IN THE SECOND AMERICAN REVOLUTION

HOW I BEAT SATAN...AND THE IRS

Video Workshops Found at vimeo.com/markemery

THE PRIVATE TRAVELLER

THE PREVIOUS TAXPAYER

PORTABLE TRADES AND OCCUPATIONS

ESCAPE THE MATRIX

STOP WITHHOLDING

DON'T ARGUE WITH THE IRS...AGREE AND BE FREE!

PRIVATE. BANKING - privatebusiness.biz

Websites

www.lighthouselaw.club

www.onefreemanswar.com

Look for Lighthouse Law Club on Social Media

YouTube.com
Minds.com
Instagram
BrightEon.com

ADVANCED FINANCIAL RESOURCES

Private Banking - privatebusiness.biz

Webinar - The Stealthy Capitalist
http://bit.ly/stealthy_capitalist_webinar

Monaco Management Group - http://MMG.world

MMG Financial Services - http://MMGFinance.com

Run Bankers Run - video series
http://bit.ly/runbankersrun

Financial Privacy - video series
http://bit.ly/secure_privacy

Made in the USA
Monee, IL
25 April 2021